The Statutes of Sir Walter Mildmay
for Emmanuel College

Queen Elizabeth I, from the charter for the foundation of Emmanuel College
(attributed to Nicholas Hilliard)
© The Master and Fellows of Emmanuel College, 1983

The Statutes of Sir WALTER MILDMAY Kt Chancellor of the Exchequer and one of Her Majesty's Privy Councillors; authorised by him for the government of EMMANUEL COLLEGE founded by him

Translated and supplied with an introduction
and commentary by FRANK STUBBINGS
Fellow and lately Librarian of the College

CAMBRIDGE UNIVERSITY PRESS

Cambridge
London   New York   New Rochelle
Melbourne   Sydney

Published by the Press Syndicate of the University of Cambridge
The Pitt Building, Trumpington Street, Cambridge CB2 1RP
32 East 57th Street, New York, NY 10022, USA
296 Beaconsfield Parade, Middle Park, Melbourne 3206, Australia

© Cambridge University Press 1983

First published 1983

Printed in Great Britain by
New Western Printing Ltd, Bristol

Library of Congress catalogue card number: 82–12960

British Library Cataloguing in Publication Data
Emmanuel College
The statutes of Sir Walter Mildmay Kt, Chancellor
of the Exchequer and one of Her Majesty's Privy
Councillors, authorised by him for the government
of Emmanuel College founded by him.
1. Emmanuel College
I. Title   II. Mildmay, *Sir* Walter
III. Stubbings, Frank H.
378.426'59   LF180
ISBN 0 521 24750 0

Coming to *Court* after he had founded his *Colledge*, the *Queen* told him, Sir *Walter*, I hear you have erected a *Puritan Foundation*. No, *Madam*, saith he, farre be it from me to countenance any thing contrary to your established Lawes, but I have set an *Acorn*, which when it becomes an *Oake*, God alone knows what will be the fruit thereof.

Thomas Fuller,
History of the University of Cambridge (1655)

Contents

Plates

Preface

This translation of the original statutes of Emmanuel College was first made twenty years ago, with no clear intention of publication, though with the conscious thought that the contents would be interesting to others beside the translator, including those who had not the time, the patience, nor the knowledge, to read the original Latin. This I still believe, even though few readers have ferreted out the typescript laid up in the College Library unless directed to it by the translator (who happens for most of the time to have been the Librarian). Those few have included several serious historians of the sixteenth century, who doubtless would themselves have been content with the Tudor Latin version, but were glad to quote the crib for their readers.

The approach of the quatercentenary of the College's foundation has stimulated interest in the early history of Emmanuel; and I am very grateful to the College History Committee for encouraging me to get the translation into print before 1984 is upon us. The text has of course been revised, though there was fortunately little to alter. Twenty years have, however, increased my knowledge of the College and its history; and so I have ventured to add a commentary to supplement the information provided by the Statutes themselves and to explain things which I did not myself understand when I first translated them. I have also been persuaded to prefix to the Statutes some account of events and developments in the University during the lifetime of the Founder which may help towards a better appreciation of his motivation and his intentions in the creation of Emmanuel College.

Emmanuel College, July 1981   Frank Stubbings

Abbreviations

E.C.A.	Emmanuel College Archives
ECM	*Emmanuel College Magazine*
Trans. Camb. Bib. Soc.	*Transactions of the Cambridge Bibliographical Society*

Introduction

A CHARTER of Queen Elizabeth I dated 11 January in the twenty-seventh year of her reign (1583/4), which is the prime treasure among the Emmanuel College Archives, empowers Sir Walter Mildmay, Knight, Chancellor of the Exchequer and one of Her Majesty's Privy Council, to establish a 'College of sacred theology, sciences, philosophy, and good arts' consisting of a Master and thirty Fellows and Scholars (graduate and undergraduate), more or less. The College is to be a perpetual body corporate, with the usual powers of owning property, and of suing and being sued in the courts of the realm; and the Founder (or after him his heirs or assigns) is authorised to make statutes for the good and wholesome governance and regulation of the College. It is the statutes made by Sir Walter under this charter that are here presented in full in an English translation. As a picture of a living society a body of rules might well be thought no more than dry bones; but Mildmay's statutes have a deal more flesh on them than their modern counterparts. He is not afraid to explain his motives, and that not only in the preface, which sets the tone of the College as a seminary of Puritan preachers. Nor is the text cast all in large and general words. In these statutes we read not only what manner of men the Founder wanted as Master and Fellows and Scholars, but also what faults and vices they were to avoid; not only how their election was to be conducted but what possible malpractices must be guarded against. Allowances for food and clothing, fines for lateness or neglect of duty, are specified to the last halfpenny. We meet here not only the dons and the undergraduates, but even the under-cook and the laundryman.

Not everything, of course, could be covered; day-to-day detail of, say, the times of meals or (more important) the prescribed books for lectures or the surveillance of undergraduate behaviour, had to be left to the discretion of the Master and other College officers; but for these matters we are happily able to supplement the Statutes by a body of College orders of 1588 which codified the practices that had developed in the first three years of running the new society. These orders are printed, with some explanatory comments, after the Statutes.

The classic recipe for making yoghurt begins: *Take some previous yoghurt* . . . So Sir Walter Mildmay, drawing up statutes for his new College, looked to those of Christ's College, where he had himself been an undergraduate some forty-five years earlier, and where Laurence Chaderton, the intended Master of Emmanuel, had been a Fellow. It is worth noting here that the Christ's statutes, drawn up in 1505, had themselves been based on those of the parent foundation of God's House (1439), though with much amplification and with a more classical Latinity. Those of God's House had in turn been based on those of Clare Hall (1359). (These earlier documents may best be consulted in *Early Statutes of Christ's College . . . with the statutes of God's House*, edited with an introduction, translation, and notes by H. Rackham, and printed for Christ's College in 1927; and in *Documents relating to the University and Colleges of Cambridge*, published by the Universities Commission, 3 vols., London, H.M.S.O., 1852.) The divergences from the Christ's model will appear more particularly from the commentary which has been appended to each chapter. It is intended that this commentary should be read as an essential part of the present volume, rather than being reserved like footnotes for reference only in special need. To this extent it is hoped that the body of the book will be self-explanatory; but the intentions of the Founder, and his means of achieving them, cannot be fully appreciated without some consideration of the larger historical setting.

(a) The statute-book.   (b) Opening page of the Statutes.

1. (a) The statute-book.

2. The end of chapter 42, with the Founder's signature, and (opposite) the witnesses' signatures and certificate.

(b) The Founder's seal, with his quarterly arms.

3. (a) Base of the silver seal-box, with the arms of Mildmay (Gloucestershire).

Anno Dni 1588. Decemb. 10.

This order & Conference before written, with the manner of & using the same, is ordayned & appointed to bee continually, observed by common consent of the Mr and the fellowes, as by carets be/ ~~their hyndes~~ _their handes. Anno Dni. 1588. Decemb. 10._

Laurence Chaderton.
Charles Chadwick
William Iones
Laurs Pickeringe
Iohn Cook.
Iohn Richardson.
Nathaniel Gylbie.
William Branthwayte.
William Bright.
Iohn Graye.
Thom Duke.
Richard Rolfe.
Robert Houghton.

4. Signatures of the first twelve Fellows to the College orders of December 1588.

The historical background

I *A Puritan college*

At its foundation, and for three-quarters of a century thereafter, Emmanuel was often commented on as different from other Cambridge colleges, as a 'Puritan' college, where the Chapel lay north and south, not east and west, where they wore no surplices and received the Holy Communion sitting; they were Calvinists, they were Presbyterians, they were nonconformists, they were (it was implied) disloyal to church and state. That these criticisms all concerned matters of churchmanship was fair enough, for the Founder's prime purpose was to establish a place for the education and training of ministers of the church; yet they were facile and often shallow, and there is, and always was, much that could be said in reply. Viewed historically, the orientation of the Chapel (and other College buildings) had as much to do with the bearing of the Roman road through Cambridge as it had with disapproval of Romanist tradition; subsequent history shows that surplices may come and go – and their last disappearance from Emmanuel undergraduates at prayer was in deference to no scruple about ritual but to the exigences of wartime clothes-rationing; and Laurence Chaderton, the first Master, when asked at the 1604 Hampton Court conference what he had to say about 'sitting communions', replied that it was 'by reason of the seats so placed as they be', but that they had some kneeling also. His response is important not only as evidence that Puritans were not devoid of humour; it typifies Chaderton's view that externals are in the true analysis things indifferent, and that variation should therefore be tolerated in either direction. As to the supposed political implications of nonconformity, no one could have been more loyal or less revolutionary than the Founder, a skilled administrator who occupied positions of increasing responsibility and trust under each monarch from Henry VIII to Elizabeth I. His college was not designed to promote an 'alternative' church, but to improve the quality of clergy within the existing framework; and Chaderton, whom he personally chose as Master, is on record as saying that he would give his right hand rather than countenance anything contrary to the Queen's established laws. This is not to deny that both were men of strong religious convictions, and that both favoured reform rather than reaction; but change was not something to be forced; the right seed with right nurture would in God's good time grow as it ought. The Founder's famous analogy of planting an acorn is no mere witticism; it sums up a whole philosophy.

We are not in a position to trace the development of the Founder's own religious beliefs. He was born (around 1520) in an England which was still Roman Catholic, though the sparks of reformation were already kindling among the more learned and spiritual; his foundation of Emmanuel towards the end of his life – when a man's inner convictions tend to assert themselves most clearly – reveals him plainly in the Puritan camp, though we must remember that 'Puritan' is a label, normally, of disapprobation, with undertones and implications of an extremism which 'wise, grave Mildmay' never shared. But although his spiritual odyssey is unrecorded we may perhaps divine something of it from the events and circumstances of his lifetime. His services in government, to economic and parliamentary administration, were undoubtedly great; but his foundation of Emmanuel may well have seemed to him – as perhaps it was absolutely – the most important thing he ever did. To assess such a claim one needs to see not only the character of the College as revealed by its statutes, but its position in relation to the dramatic vicissitudes and development of both the church and the University through much of the sixteenth century; to look back, in fact, as Mildmay might himself have done, over events which he had himself lived through, or at furthest heard of from men of his father's generation.

II Reformation and secularisation in Cambridge

J. B. Mullinger, in his history of the University of Cambridge, made the royal injunctions of Henry VIII in 1535 the dividing event between the mediaeval and the modern University. The injunctions were of cardinal importance in the secularisation of the University; where it previously owed allegiance first to the Pope and next to the King, henceforth its allegiance must be to the King alone, as head of both church and state. But their specific provisions gave effect to trends in theology and academic study which had already been developing for thirty years or more. The dethronement of ecclesiastical authority represented by their abolition of degrees in canon law went deeper in the provision that theological lectures were no longer to be according to the scholastic commentators, but 'according to the true sense' of Scripture, and that students were to be permitted and encouraged to study the Bible for themselves. But direct interpretation of holy writ needed to be backed by learning; and there was a further regulation that the Colleges must provide daily lectures in Latin and Greek. The latter had been taught in the University at least since the residence of Erasmus at Queens' (1511–1514) and the establishment of the Lady Margaret Readership (1502), both under the aegis of John Fisher as Chancellor. The publication in 1516 of Erasmus's own new recension and translation of the Greek New Testament had been a landmark in the theological application of the 'new learning'; and long before the King's breach with the Pope the humanists had been criticising the academic traditions of the universities as stale and sterile. But the 1535 injunctions continued to recognise the education of the clergy as the main, or at least a major, function of the universities, and a necessary and desirable one at that, especially if the clergy (as they had done throughout the Middle Ages) were not only to fulfil the priestly and pastoral functions of the church but to provide leading figures in the government of the country. In addition, it had long been the practice of the monastic establishments to 'exhibit' some of their number to the University for the furtherance of their studies, quite apart from the existence of monasteries or friaries of the principal orders in Cambridge itself; and in the same year as the injunctions a statute was passed which made it actually obligatory upon at least the major abbeys each to maintain two men in study at the universities. At the same time there is evidence that some found the charms of academe too alluring. Beneficed clergy liked to prolong their stay in Cambridge beyond the needs of study; and in 1536 there were further provisions, both that those who were not seriously working for a degree should return to their cures, and also that the wealthier clerics should at their own expense maintain poorer younger men in the University who might later assist them in their pastoral charge. (Fifty years later, Mildmay could still feel that the hungry sheep looked up and were not fed, though the pabulum he believed they needed was of a different order.)

Despite these measures of the mid-1530s the strongly knit links between church and university were already breaking up. Men like Erasmus or Fisher had hoped to use the new learning as a force to purify and revivify the doctrine and life of the church. More widely, however, it was seen as a challenge to the entrenched tradition of ecclesiastical authority: and at the same time humanism was developing as an alternative and secular system of education. Study in the university came to be regarded as the means to a *layman*'s career in public life. Higher education was the way to a rapidly increasing range of government offices, and so to affluence and a stake in the country. The years between the break with Rome and the accession of Queen Elizabeth I are the period when this distinction between ecclesiastic and civil employment became clearly drawn. The separation was indeed encouraged even from within the church; Latimer urged that laymen should take on the administrative work of the realm so that the clergy might devote themselves to their proper pastoral and preaching duties.

An associated effect was a change in the social origins of those attracted to the University. Where the typical student had been a poor man seeking a career in the church, there was by the 1540s a larger proportion of sons of the nobility and gentry whose parents recognised the cultural value of literary studies;

> ingenuas didicisse fideliter artes
> emollit mores, nec sinit esse feros.

This change was bound up, in the inenubilable interchange of cause and effect, with developments in the character of the Colleges and their status within the University. It was in general true that the earlier colleges were founded for the nurture of poor scholars intended for the priesthood. Other students lived more independently, with lesser commitment to discipline, in student hostels which had neither the permanency of a corporate community nor its comprehensive concern for the welfare and instruction of its members. The organisation of teaching and learning, by lectures and disputations, had been the concern of the University authorities, not the Colleges. The sixteenth century saw gradual and sometimes startling growth in the endowment, the functions, and the influence of the Colleges in Cambridge, and the consequent eclipse of the once numerous hostels. Here again we should look to the beginning of the century for the initiation of these changes, which were only partially foreseen by those most concerned. When John Fisher in 1506 persuaded the Lady Margaret Beaufort, the widowed mother of King Henry VII, to devote her wealth and influence to the refoundation of God's House as Christ's College, and again in 1511 to found St John's College on the dying embers of the former Hospital of the Knights of St John, he doubtless had the same purposes in mind as he had in bringing Erasmus to Cambridge: to exploit new trends in learning to the benefit of the Catholic Church. But there were new trends in organisation too. The College statutes of Christ's (and those of St John's were almost identical) were the first to make specific provision for the study of the ancient poets and orators; they were also the first to make specific mention of *pensioners* within the College – students, that is, who were not supported by the charitable endowment, but paid for their own sustenance, and though not members of the corporate society enjoyed along with the Scholars its concern for their welfare, physical, educational, and spiritual. The availability of such concern was naturally a powerful factor in deciding a family to commit its teen-age sons to the possible temptations of student status. A youth of wealth or noble birth might enter as a Fellow-Commoner and share the table and to some degree the society of the Fellows; but whether Fellow-Commoner or pensioner he would be under the care of a tutor, normally a Fellow of the College, who in the words of a later writer was expected to guide him to 'learning by instruction and virtue by example', but also had a duty to the College to see that the pupil's bills were met. This practice was not new, but from this time on it gained wider currency and recognition. College responsibility for teaching also became progressively more normal; we have already seen that by 1535 the royal injunctions made the provision of regular College lectures on both Latin and Greek obligatory.

III *Mildmay and Cambridge in the 1530s*

It was to Christ's College that the young Walter Mildmay was sent, about the year 1538. No record of the precise date of his admission survives; and as he took no degree, we do not know precisely when he left Cambridge either, though there is evidence that he was in London by 1540. He was a first-generation university entrant; his father was a substantial citizen of Chelmsford in Essex (an area near enough to London to be well in touch with the fashions and opportunities of the day), but of no academic background. His elder brother Thomas had already by 1535 a position as auditor in the Office of First Fruits and Tenths, which handled revenues arising from the 1534 statute annexing clerical taxation to the Crown; and we later find him employed in making inventories of the possessions of the dissolved monasteries. With the profits of such official employment Thomas was able to purchase the Essex manor of Moulsham (once the property of the Abbey of Westminster). The Mildmay family was thus typical of the *novi homines* of that age, for whom office was the means to land-owning status, and for whom a university education came to seem a useful preparation for public service.

What the young Walter made of life at Christ's we do not know. The Master, Henry Lockwood, who held that office from 1530 to 1548, was on friendly terms with Thomas Cromwell, then Chancellor of the University. The College chapel was rich with stained glass and finely carved stonework, with gilt crucifix, candlesticks, and chalice garnished with pearls and precious stones; and the Statutes required regular attendance at masses dignified with all the pomp of copes and vestments of cloth of gold and gorgeous velvets. A new organ had been installed in 1532. But on another level Cambridge had long been deeply stirred by the Protestant ferment. It was twelve years since Dr Robert Barnes, prior of the Augustinian Friary (on the site more recently occupied by the Arts School and the Cavendish Laboratory), had preached in St Edward's a famous reforming sermon that led to his trial for heresy. A few years after that the young Thomas Bilney, whose Protestant fervour had so influenced Latimer, had similarly been summoned to Westminster to answer to Cardinal Wolsey for his views. Since then, the debate over the royal divorce and the King's rejection of the papal authority had given religious controversy a new political dimension; and the 1535 injunctions were a still fresh warning that the University and Colleges would do well to watch their step. When Mildmay matriculated the monks and friars were still on the Cambridge stage; it was not five minutes' walk from Christ's to the Franciscans (where Sidney Sussex now stands) and two hundred yards in the opposite direction the Dominicans could be seen going in and out of their long church in what was called, from their presence, Preachers' Street. He was probably still an undergraduate at the time of the dissolution of the monasteries; and it could (though this is conjecture) have been the consequent doubts whether the Colleges might not be threatened with similar extinction (though the optimistic hoped to gain something from the property and revenues of the dissolved houses) that persuaded Mildmay to quit Cambridge.

Though Christ's College as yet showed none of the Puritan bias for which it was notorious forty years later, Mildmay must have been as aware as anyone else of the conflict of beliefs and consciences that underlay the outward events. Even within the College he may have met with the young Edmund Grindal (one day to be archbishop and in conflict with Queen Elizabeth I over the manifestations of reformed religion), who spent a brief spell at Christ's before migrating to Pembroke, where on graduating B.A. he was promptly elected a Fellow and became the right-hand man of Nicholas Ridley.

Mildmay's vocation, however, was not to the church or to scholarship. Within a few years he was profitably employed in the Court of Augmentations which handled the monastic lands and revenues appropriated to the Crown; but like many thousands of alumni through the centuries he had acquired, and retained, an affection for Cambridge and for his college which was to show later in practical ways.

IV The Dissolution and the Colleges

The Cambridge anxiety over the future of the Colleges engendered by the suppression of the monasteries and chantries was happily short-lived. Henry VIII, like his successors, showed himself no enemy to the universities, provided they were loyal to the Crown; rather they were to be strengthened and improved as a bastion of the new structure of church and state. The teaching strength of Cambridge was augmented in 1540 by the endowment of five Regius Professorships – in Divinity, Civil Law, Physic, Hebrew, and Greek; and though the chair of Divinity was filled by a virtual nonentity (probably for fear that a more distinguished man like Nicholas Ridley or Matthew Parker might prove a storm-centre) the appointment of Thomas Smith to that of Civil Law and of John Cheke to that of Greek showed proper recognition of two of the best scholars of the age.

Cheke, a Fellow of St John's still under thirty, was one of a group known for their advanced views, and it was probably for fear that successful innovation in Greek studies might embolden him to the open promotion of new-fangled ideas in theology too that led the Chancellor (Stephen Gardiner, the somewhat reactionary Bishop of Winchester) to pounce upon him so promptly in the famous controversy over the pronunciation of ancient Greek which followed soon after his appointment.

The spoliation of the monasteries soon yielded further gains to the University in the creation of two new colleges. The first was the refoundation, as Magdalene College, of the old Buckingham College, which had been principally a home from home for Benedictines studying in Cambridge; and the new endowment came from Thomas Audley, newly created Lord Audley of Walden, one of the wealthiest of those who had acquired former monastic estates. His executors, to whom it fell to draw up statutes for the College, included two Roman Catholics; and the statutes were not finally sanctioned until the reign of Queen Mary. Whatever, therefore, were the Founder's designs, they show no preference for the new learning or for reformed religion, and are per-haps deliberately reticent in indicating what direction the intellectual life of the College should take. They are notable, however, as Mullinger pointed out, for the self-contained character of the constitution they embody. The Master was to be appointed by the Lord of Audley End, as representative of the Founder; and he was to have unusually com-plete powers over the College and its Fellows, without appeal to any outside authority.

But existing colleges were in a poor way financially, and fears for their future reached a peak with the 1545 'Act for the dissolution of colleges'. At this critical juncture it appears that Cambridge was par-ticularly fortunate to have good friends at court: Thomas Smith, who had recently been appointed clerk of the council to Queen Catherine Parr, and John Cheke, who was now acting as tutor to the young Prince Edward. The result of the royal commission's enquiry into the state of the Colleges which followed in 1546 was not the dreaded dissolution, but a new foundation more glorious than had ever before been envisaged. The King's new College of the Undivided Trinity incorporated and (though it used much of their buildings) virtually engulfed the two earlier foundations lying between Gonville and Caius and St John's – Michaelhouse and King's Hall. The old home of the Cambridge Franciscans was vigorously exploited for stone for the new college; its water supply was intercepted, and still today feeds the fountain in Trinity's Great Court. The new college was richly endowed with revenues from the tithes impropriated over the years by the friars. For its first Master (John Redman) and several of its early Fellows it drew freely upon St John's, to the extent that Roger Ascham (himself a Johnian) was able to state that it was but a *colonia deducta* from that college not only for its personnel but for 'both order of learning and discipline of maners'.

Just how much is implied by the last phrase is hard to judge; perhaps no more than would be inevitable in a new college with an ex-Johnian Master. We do know from ample testimony in the letters of Roger Ascham that St John's led the University in the 1530s and 1540s in classical scholarship. We know too that it was as much a home of the new theology as of the new learning, where young dons were as warm in their argument about the nature of the mass as about the beauties of Sophocles or Isocrates, as ready to raise a voice in public against the Pope (and that under a papist Master) as to put on a Christmas play in the original Greek of Aristophanes rather than a home-made Latin imitation of Plautus or Terence.

Direct evidence of life in Trinity is less readily available; but something of it may be learned from its original statutes. As these were not promulgated until 1552, and were revised in the second year of Elizabeth I (1560), they may be presumed to represent already established practice as well as intention. Compared with those of St John's (which were virtually identical with those of the Lady Margaret's other foundation, Christ's) they are remarkably full and detailed. Mullinger commented, perhaps rather unjustifiably, on Fisher's supposed intention of immutability in that earlier code; but the Trinity Statutes, if they were observed to the letter, are a deal more inflexible in that they attempt to legislate for almost every detail of daily life and activity, from the words of the collect to be spoken by the undergraduate when he knelt by his bed on waking through the daily timetable of lectures and prescribed books, Chapel services, the yearly sequence of academic exercises on his route to a degree, and even his obligatory participation in the Christmas holiday play-acting. The religious character of the College is emphatic. At least one quarter of the Fellows were to be preachers, and to deliver a specified quota of sermons within and without the College. The 1560 revision states that it was indeed the prime purpose of the foundation (had there already been some falling off?) to maintain men in the study of holy Scripture and to train them for the teaching of the faith. The Fellows must give an undertaking to seek holy orders at due time after graduation, or to relinquish their place. Requirements as to the character and discipline of Fellow-Commoners and pensioners are strict; and the duties of tutors and pupils are specifically stated.

All of this is of importance when we come to examine the intentions of Sir Walter Mildmay's foundation and the Emmanuel Statutes. Most important of all, perhaps, is the oath to be taken on appointment or election at Trinity by Master, Fellows, and Scholars alike. As at Christ's or St John's it included an undertaking to keep the Statutes and to respect and further the interests of the College; but that was now preceded by solemn promises sincerely to embrace the Christian faith, always taking holy Scripture rather than man-made rules or traditions as the essential guide in faith and morals; and to acknowledge the supreme authority of the Crown in all human affairs, independent of the jurisdiction of any foreign bishop. If there was implied a new freedom in the interpretation of Scripture, yet in church polity there must be uniformity. The next few decades were to exhibit these two principles in collision.

V Conflict and crisis

In sum, the intention of the Trinity Statutes was little different from that of the royal injunctions of 1535; but the immediate development of the University took directions not envisaged by statutes. The improved opportunities of a secular education were clearly more widely attractive than a career in a church whose doctrines were still the subject of fundamental controversy; and as the University became fashionable for the well-to-do, there were inevitably some who came to it for no other reason than that it was the fashion. Roger Ascham was by 1547 writing that Cambridge was all too full of rich men's sons who had neither the desire to become priests and preachers nor any real bent for learning. Latimer deplored the poor supply of educated clergy from the University; John Caius, returning to Cambridge in 1558 after a considerable absence, complained that discipline was poor, and that the students were largely gentlemen and idlers. The sympathies of Caius were Catholic, and his memory went back to the days before the Dissolution. But Martin Bucer, the Strasburg reformer brought to Cambridge in 1549 as Regius Professor of Divinity, was no less severe in his comment that the Colleges, endowed for education of the clergy, were now occupied by dons who had adopted all the more deplorable characteristics of the old-time denizens of the abbeys, to the exclusion of the more worthily studious, or the corruption of those who did enter the University.

The appointment of Bucer, the doyen of the continental reformers, had, in H. C. Porter's phrase, 'set the seal upon the success of the Cambridge reformers'; and for some the *Book of Common Prayer* of 1549 might be seen in the same light. But there were others, neither few nor silent, for whom the new book was too moderate, and for whom the retention of prayers for the dead, vestments, the sign of the cross, and other ritual acts of devotion still smacked intolerably of Popery. The second book, of 1552, did much to meet them, and there was a wholesale purge of vestments and Chapel furnishings in the Colleges. Some were sold, others just stored away, to be triumphantly or reluctantly brought out again a year later with the official restoration of Roman practice under Queen Mary.

It has sometimes been claimed that the conflict of the Reformation has never been finally fought out in England; yet in many ways the five years of Mary's reign were crucial in bringing controversy to the ultimate test of conscience for individual churchmen. Some twenty-five senior members of the University of Cambridge died for their convictions, including such leaders as Thomas Cranmer, John Bradford, Nicholas Ridley, and Hugh Latimer, while many others went into exile, and a few like Matthew Parker remained in hiding. But we should doubtless be wrong to assume that others who were not called upon to suffer publicly were therefore indifferent. 'One suffering for the truth', wrote Latimer, 'turneth more than a thousand sermons.' What, for example, are we to suppose was the effect of the Marian martyrdoms on a man like Sir Walter Mildmay? He remained in public service throughout Mary's reign, though he no longer sat in the Commons in her later Parliaments. Yet his religious position was never in doubt; and his partiality for the Puritan cause, so evident later, may well have matured at this time. *Render unto Caesar* . . . is not a text of mere time-serving pragmatism. Better the pinch of conscience over matters ultimately indifferent than open discord and the shedding of innocent blood. The excesses of Mary's reign strengthened the view – shared in the sixteenth century by most Protestants as well as most Catholics – that uniformity in religion was essential to the welfare and order of society. But what uniformity?

VI The progress of Puritanism

In the 1560s and 1570s there was increasingly open expression of the Puritan view that the church, though rescued from the oppressions of Popery, had still not returned as it ought to the purity of primitive Christianity. Three lines of approach may be distinguished; theological, ritual and organisational. On the theological plane the main issues were the doctrines of justification by faith, and of predestination; and the nature of the Eucharist. As to ritual, there were still those who inveighed against all church vestments and many details of ritual practice – issues to promote undergraduate demonstration, as they did, but regarded by the moderates as things indifferent. The third issue, of church organisation, was the one that must eventually provoke more serious confrontation with authority. Many Puritans held that the primitive church was shown by Scripture to have been Presbyterian. Archbishops and bishops therefore must go; ministers should be elected by their congregations for their pastoral and preaching capacities (and it followed that they must never be pluralist or non-resident); uniformity between congregations should be ensured by conference in provincial synods, headed by a general synod.

In Cambridge the chief proponent of these views was Thomas Cartwright, Fellow of Trinity and Lady Margaret Professor of Divinity, whose lectures in 1569–70 provoked official repression. Fear of his popularity, and the risk of an avowed Puritan being elected Vice-Chancellor, led John Whitgift, the Master of Trinity, in consultation with William Cecil as Chancellor, to obtain a revision of the University Statutes. The new Statutes of 1570 gave greater powers to the Vice-Chancellor and heads of houses to restrain 'unruly' Fellows; and they made the heads responsible for seeing that disputations and lectures on the statutorily prescribed subjects and books were held regularly in individual colleges. Thus without unduly cramping freedom of expression, at least some balance of doctrine might be maintained in the instruction available in Cambridge, instead of having all students alike running after a Puritan professor.

None the less, the Puritan cause gained sufficient strength to promote in 1572 a formal *Admonition to Parliament* advocating a Presbyterian reconstitution of the Church of England. The consequence of the failure of this appeal was the establishment of a shadow Presbyterian organisation on an unofficial basis, a sort of church within the church. The situation has indeed its more modern parallels. The leaders of the Puritan movement were, naturally enough, in frequent contact with each other; often their families were related by marriage. It was easy enough in practice for like-minded parochial clergy to meet together in a *classis* or synod for discussion and exchange of views, and (for they were utterly sincere in basing their views on Scripture) for study and interpretation of the Bible. This last (known in the parlance of the day as 'prophesying') was of basic importance. But if they held that the

Spirit might speak through any sincere believer, that did not mean that all interpretations were equally valid. There must be uniformity in truth, even if the means to truth were not all equally perfect. Hence the need for the *classis* and the prophesying meeting; hence also the need to appeal from time to time to the Puritan leaders in the University for their more learned advice, either by correspondence or actually by sending delegates for annual conference at Stourbridge Fair time in September. It is difficult to fault the Puritans' logic; their practices did not necessarily conflict, as the moderates recognised, with the authority of the ecclesiastical establishment; and there was without doubt too much truth in their criticism of clergy who spent their time in academic sloth in the University to the neglect of the flocks for whose spiritual care they were beneficed. On the other hand, authority might see in the *classis* movement all the risks of nonconformity – of the corruption of accepted doctrine and the subversion of established church order, perhaps even of civil order.

The need for more parochial clergy who had the education and the call to preach was something that was increasingly recognised not only by Puritans, but by the Bishops themselves. While Matthew Parker was archbishop (1559–75) the 'prophesying' meetings spread but slowly; but his successor, Edmund Grindal, was sympathetic to them. His appointment had been warmly recommended by Burghley, who perhaps hoped that through him the Queen might be persuaded to such moderate changes as might satisfy some of the Puritans' aspirations. At the same time, he was not likely to encourage the extremists; we may recall that as Archbishop of York Grindal had been much upset by Cartwright's controversial pronouncements, and had as a result intervened to oppose his admission to the degree of Doctor of Divinity. But Grindal's approval of 'prophesyings' brought him into direct conflict with the Queen, who was persuaded that they held the seeds of tumult and rebellion. Grindal consulted the Bishops, and found that eight were in favour to four against; but the Queen was 'so moved against those exercises that downe she woulde have them', and commanded Grindal to have them suppressed. He stood his ground, protesting that he had not the legal power to do this against the will of the other Bishops; and also that without such exercises as the 'prophesyings' the clergy would remain unlearned and unfit to preach; and if the Queen was against preaching, and believed that reading printed homilies could take its place, then experience and even Scripture were against her. The Queen, who was as much incensed by the fact that Grindal dared to disobey as by his stubborn defence of 'prophesyings', would have liked to deprive him of his archbishopric; but the legal difficulties of depriving an archbishop were such a 'no man's land' of problems of jurisdiction that he was allowed to remain under house arrest, and never regained favour, though she relented somewhat at his end.

VII   *Mildmay and the Puritans*

It is time to return to Sir Walter Mildmay. On a superficial view one might be tempted to think that what went on in Cambridge was no interest of his, even that he might be unaware of it all. But Elizabethan England was a small world, and Mildmay as a Privy Councillor and Chancellor of the Exchequer was near the heart of it. The two universities were perhaps even more than nowadays centres of influence in the country and of prime concern to government. The Chancellor of Cambridge (and his role in University affairs was far more direct and vigorous than is expected in modern times) was from 1559 to his death in 1598 no less a man than William Cecil, Lord Burghley, the Queen's principal secretary of state. Mildmay was intimate with him socially as well as officially. The proem of Roger Ascham's *Scholemaster*, with its delightful picture of conversation at the Principal Secretary's dinnertable at Windsor in 1563, typifies the opportunities there were for such as Mildmay to be informed of events in the educational world, even when he had no official concern with them. Besides, he had personal reasons for Cambridge visits and contacts; his two sons Anthony and Humphrey were Fellow-Commoners at Peterhouse in the 1560s, and whatever the reason they did not go to their father's college, Sir Walter's continued goodwill towards Christ's is clear from his benefaction of 1568, when besides books for the library he made over an annual revenue of twenty pounds a year to maintain a Greek lecturer, a preacher, and six undergraduate scholars. Possibly Mildmay had already at that date observed at Christ's, and wished to encourage, a trend towards the Puritanism for which it was renowned in the following decade. For 1568 was the year in which Edward Dering, a leader in that trend, became a senior Fellow, and Laurence Chaderton, another convinced though always moderate and eirenical Puritan, was first elected. In any case, there need be no doubt that Mildmay was well informed of events and movements in Cambridge.

As to the spread of Puritanism in the country generally, he was not merely interested, but directly involved on the government side over the matter of 'prophesyings'. There is good evidence (it has been well presented by S. Lehmberg in his *Sir Walter Mildmay and Tudor Government*, Univ. of Texas, 1964) that Mildmay followed the situation closely. He was sympathetic to the practice, but with Burleigh endeavoured to persuade Grindal to moderate his stand against the Queen, foreseeing that any action so drastic as the deprivation of his archbishopric on this issue would boost the 'pride and practice of the papists' besides unnecessarily antagonising the Puritans. There can be no doubt that Mildmay desired sincerely the increase of a godly and learned ministry; but he eventually concluded that the establishment of 'prophesyings' by any but the royal authority must be deleterious to church and civil order. They were not required by scriptural authority, and must be relegated to the rank of matters indifferent – harmless but not *necessary*, and therefore not to be used without full authority. Whatever his private views of their usefulness, loyalty to the Crown must be paramount.

VIII The founding of Emmanuel

Mildmay's position in all this is very relevant to his intentions in the founding of Emmanuel. That his prime purpose was the education of a preaching clergy we have his own express avowal in the preface to the College Statutes. This need had been recognised, as we have seen, by earnest churchmen of varying shades of opinion through all the vicissitudes of the preceding four decades. The *classis* movement and the exercises of 'prophesying' were directed to that end among the clergy already ordained. But the new college was to supply a new generation of ministers. As to the means, scarcely anything really new is actually laid down in Mildmay's Statutes. The existing framework of University and College organisation and instruction, hammered out over the centuries, could suffice. In most respects, as will appear in detail below, the Statutes closely followed those of Christ's, where Mildmay himself had been an undergraduate and where, he knew, in recent years it had been made plain that Puritan religion could flourish and be propagated within the college model. But it is perhaps important to notice that the Emmanuel Statutes do not appoint any external visitor. Some few issues might conceivably come to a point of internal disagreement on occasion, and for such cases there is provision for outside arbitration. But these are exceptions. In general, government of the College was to be self-contained. Details of order and instruction, Mildmay recognised, might vary from time to time; and unlike the framers of the Trinity Statutes he preferred to leave such details to the discretion of the Master and Fellows.

That, of course, made the choice of persons supremely important; and during his lifetime they were to be selected by the Founder himself. After his death he must rely on them for a continuity of similar choice; on the quality and character required of those to be subsequently elected as Scholars, Fellows, or Master, the Statutes are therefore emphatic; and all were to be bound by solemn oath to observe the requirements of the Statutes. With these precautions, any necessary changes in the future could be safely committed to them. It may well be that the most important lesson Mildmay drew from the history of the University in his own time was just this, that it was not so much the rules and regulations that mattered, as the spirit of the men who lived under them and by them. The tactical and strategic needs of government had taught him too to distinguish the essential and permanent from the transitory and indifferent. Churches could err; men might persecute and burn each other for differences of dogma and ritual; but the scriptural basis of Christianity was permanent, and man's spiritual needs were perennial. Even the modern historian of the age, diagnosing in the England of the 1580s an utterly different world from that of the 1530s, may too easily forget that there were plenty of men who like Mildmay lived in both. It is symbolic – and perhaps no chance either – that Mildmay's college for the training of a preaching clergy was planted on a site once occupied by the Dominican order of Preachers. Mildmay could have listened to them in his youth; their last prior, Gregory Dodds, ended his days as Elizabethan Dean of Exeter; and when Emmanuel was founded John Scory, the last pre-Reformation Dominican to take a Cambridge degree, was still alive as Bishop of Hereford.

The intended character of the new college was summed up, even more than in the Statutes, in the character of the first Master, Laurence Chaderton. Without him as Master, said Mildmay, he would rather found no college. Chaderton, born about 1538, entered Christ's College in 1562, where, despite a staunchly Catholic upbringing and his father's disapproval, he turned to Calvinism. He was an excellent scholar in Latin, Greek, and Hebrew, and became a distinguished theologian and a highly successful preacher at St Clement's church in Cambridge. As a Fellow of Christ's from 1568 to 1577 (when he married) he was probably the most influential personality in making Christ's, in Patrick Collinson's phrase, 'a Puritan seminary in all but name'. As more fully discussed below (see the note on the College order for 'mutuall conference') he had developed a systematic programme of Bible study and discussion for the training of ministers, which is perhaps our best evidence for the methods of the 'prophesyings' among parochial clergy which so distressed Queen Elizabeth. Chaderton was in no sense an extremist, and for all his Puritan ardour was at one with Mildmay in his attitude to 'matters indifferent' in worship, as he was in his desire for conformity to church order as by law established. In short he was the ideal embodiment of Mildmay's intentions. Had he been still a Fellow of Christ's, it is conceivable that Mildmay might have felt that his ends could be attained within the framework of the old college; and it is possible, though the evidence is by no means clear, that Mildmay may have hoped to see Chaderton elected Master of Christ's when the office fell vacant in 1581. In any case, a new college gave freer scope for the training of clergy of the kind both Chaderton and Mildmay (and many of Mildmay's influential friends) most wished to see – godly, learned, able to preach, and committed to the pastoral care. This last was to be ensured by what proved the only really controversial statute of the new foundation – that entitled *De mora sociorum* (more fully discussed in the notes to the individual statute), which limited the tenure of a Fellowship once the holder had proceeded to the degree of Doctor of Divinity. By its position after all the rest, this statute might appear an afterthought; but its content shows – and there is good external evidence too – that it was central to the Founder's purpose. Emmanuel was not to be a permanent home for scholars. The clergy who went out from Emmanuel must indeed be learned; but learning was not to be an end and profession in itself. Nor must it be merely formal and traditional. Above all, they must be thoroughly grounded in the Bible. Tradition was important, but the interpretation of Scripture was to be seen as a continuing process; spiritual insight could be vouchsafed to the present generation as well as to the apostles or prophets of old. That is the sense in which Emmanuel was to be, as the Founder states in his preface, a school of prophets. That is why, in the College orders of 1588 which round off the present volume, so much care and thought was devoted to the regulation (and the justification) of that 'communication of gifts among students of divinity' which Mildmay's contemporaries, whether for praise or disparagement, were accustomed to call 'prophesying'.

BIBLIOGRAPHICAL NOTE

The above survey makes no claim to be a work of original research, and the historian of the period will readily recognise to what secondary sources it is inevitably indebted. The principal works used are as follows:

Collinson, Patrick. *The Elizabethan Puritan movement*, London, 1967
Cross, Claire. *The Puritan Earl*, London, 1966
Curtis, Mark H. *Oxford and Cambridge in transition 1558–1642*, Oxford, 1959
Dillingham, William. *Vita Laurenti Chadertoni*, 1700: translated (not the whole text) in E. S. Shuckburgh, *Laurence Chaderton, D.D. . . .*, Cambridge, 1884
Documents relating to the University and Colleges of Cambridge, 3 vols.,London, H.M.S.O., 1852
Kearney, Hugh. *Scholars and gentlemen: universities and society in pre-industrial Britain 1500–1700*, London, 1970
Lake, Peter. *Moderate Puritans and the Elizabethan church*, Cambridge, 1982
Lehmberg, S. E. *Sir Walter Mildmay and Tudor government*, Univ. of Texas, 1964
Mullinger, J. B. *The University of Cambridge*, 3 vols., Cambridge, 1873–1911
Peile, John. *Christ's College*, London, 1900
Porter, H. C. *Reformation and reaction in Tudor Cambridge*, Cambridge, 1958
  Puritanism in Tudor England [a selection of contemporary texts], 1970
Rackham, H. *Early statutes of Christ's College*, Cambridge, 1927
Rolph, Rebecca S. 'Emmanuel College and the Puritan movements of old and new England', Ph.D. dissertation, Univ. of S. California, Los Angeles, 1979
Shuckburgh, E. S. *Emmanuel College*, London, 1904

The manuscripts

The statutes made by Sir Walter were written out fair in a special book, described below, signed and sealed by him in the presence of seven witnesses on 1 October 1585, and handed over to Laurence Chaderton, the first Master of the College. This, which we may call the Master's Book, consists of eighty leaves of vellum, $7\frac{1}{4} \times 10\frac{1}{4}$ ins., bound in oak boards covered with once crimson leather (now badly faded), with green silk ties with silver clasps. The corners of the clasps are engraved with a tiny acorn motif. The seal is attached on a plaited green and silver cord sewn into the binding and hanging from the foot of the spine. It shows the Mildmay arms: Quarterly (1 and 3) argent three lions rampant azure (Mildmay of Gloucestershire) and (2 and 4) party fesswise wavy argent and sable, three greyhounds' heads erased countercoloured (Mildmay of Essex). The wax seal is contained in a circular silver box, one and a half inches in diameter, with the arms of Mildmay (Glos.) engraved on the base. There is no lid. The whole volume is contained in a washleather jacket, lined with brown linen, bound with green silk at the edges, and with green silk tassels at the four corners. This jacket fits closely over the boards (and is indeed actually attached to the front board by the silver studs on to which the clasps at the ends of the ties fit), but it is seven inches longer at the foot, so as to hang to the same length as the seal. The whole fits into a wash-leather bag with a green silk drawstring. These washleather wrappings are seemingly of later date than the binding; for the jacket would hardly have been fixed so as to hide the crimson leather permanently when that was new; and as the green ties are of the same silk as the tassels of the jacket, the ties too are presumably not original, though the silver clasps may well be.

The text is carefully written in a black-letter script, with the initials of the chapters and of the chapter-titles gilt, except for those of the two additional chapters at the end. On the inside of the back-board has been pasted down the left-hand half of a leaf of vellum which had written on it (with gilding) the opening title of the book and the beginning of the preface – perhaps a trial-sample, though it is not apparent why it should have been preserved.

This is obviously the master-copy of the Statutes, which in accordance with chapter 6 was to be kept in the College chest and to be formally handed over to each new Master on his election (chapter 11, *ad fin.*). It would doubtless also have been used at the election of Masters or Fellows or Scholars (chapters 11, 19, 32) both for the reading of the relevant passages on the qualification of candidates, and for those elected to peruse before taking their oath. It seems probable that by 1611 it was showing signs of wear, for there is an entry in the accounts for the half-year headed 23 October 1611:

> Bynding yᵉ statute book &
> velume wax & thread   5s
>   (E.C.A., BUR.8.1. p. 61).

It is not apparent whether this was a fresh binding of the original volume or only a repair.

In the following year, under 'expenses synce October 21.1612' (*ibid.* p. 66) we find:

> for wryting, parchment
> & bynding of liber exem
> plaris statuto*rum* Collegii   40s.

This was for a second copy of the Statutes, which survives in the archives (E.C.A., COL.18.2), a vellum book of 38 leaves, 7 × 10 ins., bound in reversed calf, carefully written in italic with black-letter headings and chapter-openings. At the end of the text, in a tiny script, is the note

> Scripsit Iohannes Fowle scholaris huius Coll: discipulus.
> aᵒ Dni. 1612

and on the last leaf:

> Hic liber exemplaris e statutis originalibus
> transcriptus est in usum communem
> Collegii impensis eiusdem.

A few marginalia and notes on the fly-leaves bear witness to the use of this copy down to at least the late eighteenth century. It also appears, from a number of copies dating from the seventeenth to the nineteenth century, that it became the practice for individual Fellows to have their own personal copies of the Statutes (E.C.A., COL.18.3–9).

More important than these last is another copy now in the College Archives (E.C.A., COL.18.1) written out in a paper book of sixty-five numbered leaves, 8 × 10 ins., bound in limp vellum with gilt-stamped panels and ornaments (including an acorn motif, the occurrence of which on this as well as on the clasps of the Master's Book suggests an allusion – it would be the earliest known – to the famous anecdote). This copy is written in an excellent formal italic, without decoration; and the statutes bear the autograph signature of the Founder (but without witnesses' signatures) in the same places as in the Master's Book. A handwritten label inside the front cover bears the words: *The Earl of Westmorland 1856*; and from a cutting tipped in at the back it appears that the volume was lot no. 571 in the catalogue of books and MSS sold for the twelfth Earl by Sotheby Wilkinson and Hodge on 13–14 July 1887. It was purchased by Macmillan, perhaps acting for the College, for £12.5s. There can be no doubt that this was the Founder's own copy of the Statutes, inherited directly by the Earl of Westmorland. (Sir Walter Mildmay's eldest son Sir Anthony had no male heir; his daughter Mary married Francis Fane, first Earl of Westmorland.)

For the present edition the Master's Book and the Founder's copy have been compared with each other and with the text printed in *Documents*, III, pp. 483–523, from the British Museum MS Sloane 1739. There are no significant variants in the three manuscripts, and where they differ in spelling or punctuation the Master's Book is the one that has been followed. A few of the longer statutes have been divided into shorter paragraphs for the reader's comfort.

The Statutes of Sir Walter Mildmay, Knight, Chancellor of the Exchequer and one of Her Majesty's Privy Council, authorised by him for the government of Emmanuel College, founded by him

Preface

It is an ancient institution in the Church of God, and a tradition from the earliest times, that schools and colleges be founded for the education of young men in all piety and good letters and especially in Holy Writ and Theology, that being thus instructed they may thereafter teach true and pure religion, refute all errors and heresies, and by the shining example of a blameless life excite all men to virtue. For thus we read in the sacred history that the sons of the prophets at Naioth, Gilgal, Bethel and Jericho were brought up by those great and famous prophets Samuel, Elijah and Elisha to preach the name of God and instruct the people in true religion. And it is recorded in the Acts of the Apostles that at Jerusalem there were many synagogues, belonging nigh one to every nation, to which there flowed together men from almost every part of the world as to some mart of religion and learning and virtue, among whom Saul of Tarsus (that was afterward called Paul), a most chosen instrument of the Lord and the teacher of the Gentiles, is said to have sat at the feet of the reverend Gamaliel. For men that were inspired by the divine prompting of the spirit did understand that the light of the Gospel could not be spread abroad to all posterity to the glory of God and to the salvation of men but there were created and decked out in His Church, as it were in the garden of Paradise, some seed-plots of those most noble plants of Theology and right good learning, from the which such as had grown to maturity might be transplanted to all parts of the Church, that she, being watered by their

labours, and increased by the gift of God, might come at last to a most
flourishing and blessed estate. For in like manner as the Levites were
made guardians of the fire sent down from heaven (which it was onely
lawful to use for the burning of sacrifice upon the altar), to cherish and
preserve it; so also must the true knowledge of God (like fire descended
from heaven) be preserved and cherished lest we bring other fire (belike
Popery and those other heresies that come of the earth and of the
imaginings of men) to kindle our incense before the Lord. And as those
other streams flowed out of the fountains of the garden of Eden to
water the earth; so ought schools to be opened like fountains, that,
arising out of the Paradise of God, they may as with a river of gold
water all regions of our land, yea of the whole earth, with a faith of
purest doctrine and with a life of most holy discipline. Wherefore many
men of heroic virtue among our forefathers, following the divine and
ancient institution of God's prophets, have dedicated to God and to the
Church colleges and σοφῶν ψυχῶν φροντιστήρια academies of philosophic souls; whose magnificence and princely outlay I leave unto
others that may more nearly approach to the dignity of so great
munificence to equal them, thinking it enough for myself to copy but
the virtues of them that have set us a praiseworthy example in this as
in so many other things; and so far as in me lies to propagate purity of
life and religion unto our posterity. But since there is no society so
small that it may either be orderly governed, or long endure, without
some system and discipline of laws be established for its government
and continuance, therefore shall we draw up certain edicts and statutes,
divided under their separate heads, to define all the duties of our whole
college and those particular to each; and it is our desire that all our
members be subject and obedient thereunto.

NOTES TO THE PREFACE

This preface, embodying the statement of Sir Walter Mildmay's purpose in founding
the College, is composed with a certain literary pretension not matched in the
Statutes themselves (in which the desire for legal precision has its usual effect on
style). The translator makes no further apology for his attempt to echo its manner
in Tudoresque English. It is substantially fuller than the proem to the Christ's
College Statutes, which does little more than introduce the analogy of the head and
the members which is used in the subsequent definition of the various offices and
functions of the College.

Mildmay at once makes plain that his new college is to be a 'school of prophets'
– a phrase which to the present-day reader may seem merely metaphorical, but
which in 1584 had overtones of Puritan theology and practice, as is more plainly

spelt out in the College order of 1588 concerning 'mutuall conference in communication of giftes among Students in Divinity', printed below.

Naioth, Gilgal, etc.: For the school of prophets at Naioth, probably founded by Samuel, see 1 Samuel xix. 18ff.; x. 11. Similar schools existed in the time of Elijah and Elisha at Gilgal, Bethel, and Jericho (2 Kings ii. 3,5; iv. 38; vi. 1).

Gamaliel: See Acts v. 34; xxii. 3.

Levites . . . guardians of the fire: See Leviticus vi. 9–13. Nadab and Abihu were struck dead because they had used illicit fire for sacrifice (Leviticus x. 1–2).

streams . . . out of . . . Eden: Genesis ii. 10–14.

academies of philosophic souls: The Greek phrase is from Aristophanes, *Clouds* 94 and 128, where it is used in a tone of parody of the school of Socrates.

CHAPTER I
Of the authority of the Master

And since it is right to make a beginning from the head, by which it
behoves the other members to be ruled and governed, let us first make
ordinance concerning the Master, whom we desire to be as the head
unto all the Fellows and Scholars. To Laurence Chaderton, therefore,
Bachelor of Divinity, who hath already by my authority been appointed
Master of the aforesaid College, and to all other his successors (each in
his time), we assign authority over all the Fellows and Scholars of the
same College, to govern rule correct and admonish them, and to
administer the domestic affairs of the whole College in accordance with
the present ordinances and statutes by me enacted, which follow hereafter. But it shall not be permitted to the same Laurence, nor to anyone
of his successors, without the express consent of the majority of the
Fellows then present in the University, to engage in any quarrel plea or
other action whatever in the name of the College, either himself or
through any other person; nor to alienate or let to farm any lands
tenements tithes oblations or other possessions of the same College,
whether temporal or spiritual, whether already in possession or later to
come into possession; nor to grant to any person any office fee or
pension out of the goods lands or tenements of the aforesaid College;
nor to bestow the advowsons of any churches of which the patronage
belongs to the aforesaid College; nor to undertake, confirm, or termin-
ate, any business from which discredit or inconvenience might accrue
to the said College; except by the consent of the majority of the Master
himself and the Fellows of the same College. But whatsoever shall be
performed by the majority of the aforesaid Master and Fellows, whether
in these matters aforesaid or in any others (provided it be not contrary
to our ordinances and statutes), we desire and decree that it be deemed
valid and acceptable. Emoluments accruing from individual grants we
desire to be bestowed to the public use of the College, and not to be put
in any way to private uses; provided that they admit no person as
bailiff, receiver or agent unless he has provided to the Master and
Fellows aforesaid suitable guarantors for the indemnification of the
College in that account. We also grant unto the Master aforesaid power
to regulate the times of study and of recreation of all Scholars and
pensioners at his discretion.

NOTES TO CHAPTER I

This closely follows Christ's II, even to beginning with the word *And*, which is here less appropriate than after the proem of the Lady Margaret's Statutes. For the *Custos* (Keeper) of Christ's we have *Magister* (Master); and instead of *scolares . . . tam socios quam discipulos* (both Fellow-Scholars and Pupil-Scholars) we have the more modern *socios et scholares* (Fellows and Scholars). The clause *Emolumenta quae proveniunt . . . cedere*, ensuring that special grants be put to corporate and not private use, is new, as is the last sentence empowering the Master to regulate times of work and recreation (on which see pp. 100–5 below).

Laurence Chaderton (c. 1538–1640): after a staunchly Catholic upbringing had turned to Calvinism while a young man at Christ's, the Founder's college (where he was later a Fellow). As a good scholar in Latin, Greek, and Hebrew, a distinguished theologian and very successful preacher, and for all his Puritan ardour strictly loyal to the Church of England as by law established, he was an ideal choice as Master of the new college. Indeed, Mildmay is reported to have said that without Chaderton as Master he would found no college. His life, written in Latin by William Dillingham (Master 1653–62) and published in 1700, was translated in part by E. S. Shuckburgh in *Laurence Chaderton, D.D. . . .*, Cambridge, 1884. See also §VIII of 'The historical background' above.

advowsons: As the Founder's purpose for his college was to educate Puritan ministers and preachers he was anxious that there should be suitable livings for them to go to when qualified. He himself gave the College the advowsons of Stanground and Farcet in Huntingdonshire and of Queen Camel in Somerset. Henry Hastings, third Earl of Huntingdon, who shared Mildmay's Puritan sympathies, in 1586 gave us those of Loughborough in Leicestershire and North Cadbury and Aller in Somerset; while Sir Francis Walsingham (brother of the Founder's wife) gave Thurcaston in Leicestershire in 1585. On Puritan patronage at this time see Claire Cross, *The Puritan Earl* (London, 1966).

CHAPTER 2
Of the residence of the Master

Since it behoves the head to be united with the other members, we desire and decree that neither the present Master aforesaid nor any future Master shall be absent from the College, on any other than College business, above the space of one month in any single quarter of the year, under penalty of deprivation of his Mastership, *ipso facto*. And during that time nothing shall be allocated to him from the funds of the said College for his living or other expenses. It shall however be lawful for him in matters of urgency and upon necessary business of the same College to be absent for a longer period, according as the need may require; but we lay it upon his own conscience, under God, not to try to justify or excuse his absence by any kind of pretext of College business, unless it be such as in truth may demand his long absence, unless he shall happen to be hindered by some serious illness or by forcible detention, which he shall lawfully prove before the Vice-Chancellor of the University aforesaid, or his deputy, and two resident Doctors of Divinity, of whom one at least must concur with the Vice-Chancellor for the cause to be approved, if it happen that the question of the Master's absence be raised with him by any of the Fellows. But in other cases of need which are not apparent and which the Master is unwilling to disclose, we desire that it suffice, if he shall swear in the presence of the Vice-Chancellor or his deputy and the majority of the Fellows that he had very necessary and urgent cause, for him to take out of the succeeding quarter as many days beyond the permitted one month as shall seem to him necessary, provided that in such emergency his total absence shall not exceed the space of two months within one half of any one year.

NOTES TO CHAPTER 2

This reproduces Christ's III virtually unchanged. At Christ's, grave cause justifying exceptional absence had to be proved to the Chancellor or his deputy, but by 1584 the Chancellor would commonly be non-resident, and so reference is to be made to the Vice-Chancellor. A similar difference will be found in subsequent statutes.

A College order of 11 March 1623 records that on 3 October 1622 the Fellows agreed with the new Master, John Preston, before he took his oath, that the phrase *violenta detentione* (forcible detention) in this statute referred 'aswell to a morall as a natural violence, and that the service of the Kinge or Prince (to whom he was then a sworne servaunt) was to be esteemed as a morall violence'. (E.C.A., COL.14.1.)

CHAPTER 3
Of the mode of punishment

But lest too great severity of the head should tend to the hurt of the members, we desire and decree that the Master moderate his action in all such correction as is to be administered by him by calling in the Dean and the senior Fellow (whose duties we will describe below) to hear and see whatsoever he performs in these matters, so that (whenever it may be necessary) they may be cited as suitable witnesses of the whole transaction between the Master and the person to be punished. For we desire that if such person shall consider the Master aforesaid too severe upon him, then he shall be permitted to appeal to the Vice-Chancellor of the University or his deputy. And if the Vice-Chancellor or his deputy, after both sides have been stated, and after hearing the account of the Dean and the senior Fellow, in the presence of the two most senior Doctors of Divinity (or in the absence of Doctors, of the most senior Bachelors of Divinity) and with the concurrence of one of them, shall find that such person has just cause of appeal, he shall forthwith command the Master to withdraw such unjust punishment. But if on the other hand he shall find that such person has no ground of appeal, with the concurrence of the Doctors or Bachelors assisting, then the decision of the Master previously taken against such person shall retain its force and validity. But if through fault of the appellant the cause of appeal or complaint as aforesaid shall fail to be concluded within two weeks, then we desire that the appeal be deemed null and void, and that he have no right to pursue it further. Moreover, in criminal matters, if any of the Fellows or Scholars not being content with the decision made within the College shall carry the case by way of appeal to the Vice-Chancellor, and if after the case has been heard he shall be worsted in a matter of this kind, let him be expelled from our college as one convicted of guilt and a disturber of the peace.

NOTES TO CHAPTER 3

Christ's IV, *De cohercendis improbis* (of the punishment of the wicked) was perhaps unnecessarily full in its specification of the possible offences of Fellows (ranging from heresy and treason through homicide and fornication to missing Chapel services or disputations) and is omitted for Emmanuel. This accounts for a slight inconsequentiality in the opening words of chapter 3, which closely follow Christ's v. The *mores* of Fellows are further covered by chapter 22, of Scholars by chapter 34. The final sentence, involving expulsion for those convicted on appeal, is new.

CHAPTER 4

Of the preferment of the virtuous, and of the assignment of rooms

Furthermore, as the evil ought to be restrained from wickedness by punishment, so ought the good by rewards to be encouraged in virtue. We therefore desire and decree, that the Master shall treat more kindly and considerately those whom he sees more diligent in their pursuit of religion, learning, and honesty, and so far as he can shall always give preference to the same, and (other things being equal) to those who are of greatest seniority by admission, in all matters concerning both the College and the University which may be to their advantage and credit: as in the bearing of office, whether private or public, in the bestowal of ecclesiastical benefices, and in the assignment of rooms. And we desire that four scholars shall sleep in each room, and that none other than Fellows shall have a single room to his own private use. To the Master himself for the time being we assign those rooms which we have had built for the use of the Master. Further we decree that the rent of all rooms (which shall be exacted only from pensioners) shall be devoted to the use of the College. The amount of room-rent shall be decided by the Master in consultation with the two Fellows highest in seniority.

NOTES TO CHAPTER 4

This is based on Christ's VI, except that there a Fellow did not get a room to himself unless he was of the degree of Doctor. The rooms assigned to the Master were on the two floors above the Parlour. Two Elizabethan fireplaces can still be seen there in the Welbourne Room. The Master's accommodation was increased by the addition of rooms on what is now E Staircase in 1648–9; by the building of the Gallery over the Chapel Cloister; and by further additions on the garden side in the eighteenth and early nineteenth century. A new lodge (by Blomefield) was built in 1874, and this in turn replaced by the present house (by Tom Hancock) in 1964. Since the Second World War the Gallery is no longer treated as part of the Master's Lodge.

On *pensioners* see chapter 40. Their room-rents were a very important element in the College income.

CHAPTER 5
Of the rendering of accounts

It is also proper that all the Fellows should be informed of the state of the College. We therefore resolve that twice every year, once within a month of Easter and again within another month of the feast of St Michael the Archangel, the Master shall render to all the Fellows, having been notified three days beforehand, and being then present, or to the majority of them at least, a true and faithful account of everything concerning his office and administration – what he has expended, what he has received and what remains to be received, what the College owes, and what is owed to it. At the same time he shall cause his bailiffs and agents to make their accounts; and he shall exhibit to all the said Fellows the whole contents of the treasury, all valuables and other muniments, and shall replace them again, in their presence, in the treasury, in boxes appointed for the purpose. We also desire that at every time of rendering the said accounts there shall be made by the same two indentures setting forth the state of the same College, of which we command that one be placed in the common chest along with the money itself that may remain over after the audit, and that the other be retained in the Master's own keeping. And if perchance the Master shall not render the accounts at the appointed time, or if in rendering them he shall not satisfy the Fellows, then we desire the matter to be referred to the Vice-Chancellor or to his deputy, who shall with the assistance of two Doctors of Divinity, or in their absence of the two senior Bachelors of the same, amend the incorrect part according to his discretion. We desire however that the Master be free, should he with the increase of the College revenues wish to relieve himself of the burden of collecting the said revenues and of rendering accounts in respect of them, to delegate this duty, with the consent of the majority of the Fellows, to some one of the Fellows of the aforesaid College; and we desire that the person so designated shall receive the revenues aforesaid, and shall render an account of his receipts and expenditure in that connexion, at the times assigned for the Master to report on the state of the College and to do the other things before mentioned.

NOTES TO CHAPTER 5

This follows Christ's VII, but the permission to the Master to delegate bursarial business to a Fellow is new. Chaderton availed himself of it to appoint William

Bedell as Bursar in 1601 (E.C.A., COL.9.19A). But this was probably unusual, and there was no stipend attached to the office until 1756. Even at the end of the eighteenth century the Master (Richard Farmer) was conducting such business himself.

Audit of accounts took place twice yearly until the changes of statute consequent on The 1877 Oxford and Cambridge Act, which included some provisions for uniformity of practice in Colleges' accounts. Although audit procedure has not since then been detailed in the College Statutes, there is still an annual inspection of College plate and keys.

CHAPTER 6
Of the safe keeping of property

And so that the goods of the College may be more safely and securely kept, we desire and resolve that there be in the treasury a capacious chest, which shall be called the common chest, in which shall be placed all the College's money, along with a small box appointed for the custody of the common seal, of which box the Master himself shall carry the key. And there shall be other chests in the same treasury for the keeping of valuables and other things for necessary uses; but the Master himself shall see to it that things in daily use are kept in some safe place. There shall also be in the same treasury certain deed-boxes in which we desire to be stored the charters, letters patent, confirmations, title-deeds, indentures, bonds, and other muniments pertaining to the same College, together with an inventory of all things, and these original statutes. Further there shall be three locks to each chest, with three keys of different pattern, of which the first shall be kept by the Master or his deputy, the second by the senior Fellow for the time being, the third by the keeper of the common chest, of whose duties we will speak later. We therefore desire and resolve that nothing of the things we have above enumerated shall be lent to anyone. And if ever they must be taken out for the necessary uses of the College, there shall first be drawn up by the hand of the recipient a list thereof, which must remain inside the common chest until the things themselves shall be returned intact; which we desire to be done on the next day after the completion of their necessary use; and also that every night the Master or his deputy shall take care that all doors and gates of the College are locked from eight o'clock in winter and from nine o'clock in summer, and the keys of each one handed in to him.

NOTES TO CHAPTER 6

This closely follows Christ's VIII, including the provisions as to the three separate locks and key-holders for the College chest. At Christ's another statute (xxv) had more to say of the duties and annual election of the *Custos* or *Praefectus* of the common chest; but at Emmanuel he is mentioned here only, and the cross-reference in the wording is a 'ghost'.

The original College treasury was a small room entered only from the south-east corner of the Parlour, now the Parlour lobby. The large and heavy oak chest with three locks that still stands there (now demoted to the custody of logs for the Parlour fire), if not the original one, is at least its direct successor, saved from removal (we may presume) by its weight and bulk. Some time after the construction

of the 1874 Master's Lodge the treasury and its contents were transferred to a room
on the opposite side of the passage, now the sick-bay. Since 1974 the muniments
have been given a home in a specially designed room in the new south wing of the
Library, named after the late H. S. Bennett, who did much to put them in better
order.

Early locking of the gates was doubtless a more necessary precaution when there
was no street-lighting outside the College and little artificial light even within. The
hours here mentioned were prescribed for all colleges by the 1570 University
Statutes (*Documents*, 1, p. 493).

CHAPTER 7
Of the Master's wages

And lest perchance so many labours should be borne by the Master for nothing and without reward, we desire and decree that each Master in his turn shall receive for the work of his administration, that is to say for his annual wages, twenty pounds to be paid to him each year in equal portions at the end of the two customary terms; and for clothing each year three pounds nine shillings and fourpence; also for weekly commons two shillings each week, and for his servant's wages each year twenty-six shillings and eightpence. We also assign to the Master and grant for his personal use a garden, a dovehouse, and the grazing of all lands within the precincts of the College itself, with the exception of the Fellows' orchard.

NOTES TO CHAPTER 7

Cf. Christ's IX. The payments prescribed for Emmanuel are much higher; but the Master of Christ's was allowed to hold up to two benefices with cure concurrently with the Mastership.

The practical uses of the College grounds are to be noticed. The Master's garden included approximately the area now occupied by the Master's Lodge and the space between it and Emmanuel Street. The Fellows' orchard was approximately the same space as the present Fellows' Garden; in Loggan's view (1690) it is still fairly fully planted with small trees – probably fruit-trees. The space between the Pond, the present Hostel, the boundary wall to the S.E., and the Old Court building, nowadays known as the Paddock, was probably last grazed (by sheep) during the First World War; in the Second it was cultivated for vegetables.

CHAPTER 8
Of the Master's Deputy

Now as we have permitted the Master to be absent for certain periods from the aforesaid College, it is proper that provision be made for some attorney to act during his absence. We therefore desire and resolve that, if the Master be absent, or if the Mastership be vacant, some one of the Fellows shall always be in charge: in case of absence, that person whom the Master shall appoint, and in case of vacancy that Fellow who is senior in order of admission. And either shall hold authority as his deputy for the time, and shall preside both in assembling the Fellows and in taking counsel for the honour and advantage of the College, and shall have precedence and be shown obedience as if he were Master; with the exception that neither of them shall hold any election either of Fellows or of Scholars, nor shall he assign rooms to anyone, nor seal any letters with the common seal, nor deliver to anyone letters already sealed, except only those which concern the presentation of the Master elect. And in time of vacancy the senior Fellow shall not concern himself with the collection of College rents or with the payment of debts, but someone shall be chosen out of their whole number by the vote of the majority of the Fellows to be responsible to the College in such matters, and to make provision for all things until the new Master shall be elected and admitted.

NOTES TO CHAPTER 8

This is virtually identical with Christ's x.

CHAPTER 9
Of the qualification of the new Master to be elected

It is proper that the head be suitable to the rest of the members, and provide for the same and diligently assist them. We desire therefore and decree that he who is to be elected Master of the aforesaid College be by birth an Englishman, one of whom the Fellows believe, being persuaded by certain evidence or by long experience, that he will prudently administer the domestic affairs of the College with all faithfulness, industry, zeal and integrity, that he will keep our statutes, and to the best of his ability defend the goods, lands, possessions, liberties, privileges, and every single right of the College. We also desire that no one be elected Master except he has for eight full years publicly professed the study of sacred Theology, and is commonly known for such profession, has also publicly preached the Word of the Lord, and frequently fulfilled the office of Lecturer, has been accepted into the orders of the ministry, and sincerely abhors and detests Popery, heresy, and all superstitions and errors; in short who, in his own affairs, and in those that have at any time been entrusted to him by others, shall have shown himself a man of diligence, worth, and honesty, and whose reputation among good men has not been impaired or called in question, and who has reached the thirtieth year of his age, and has for sixteen years been diligently engaged in the study of letters in the University of Cambridge. If any such be found among the Fellows of the College, we enjoin in the Lord's name that the same be elected. But if not, let such a one be sought amongst them that have at some time been Fellows of the same College. But if neither among these can a fit person of such kind be found, then it shall be permitted to choose one from Christ's College (which we desire to be given first preference), or failing that, from the whole University of Cambridge, provided that he be distinguished in endowment with the above requisite qualities and gifts.

NOTES TO CHAPTER 9

Based closely on Christ's xi. But *by birth an Englishman* is new (cf. chapter 17); so is the minimum age of thirty, and of course the 'no-Popery' clause and the preference for a Christ's man in default of a suitable member of Emmanuel; and the requisite qualifications of religion and learning are much more fully spelled out.

CHAPTER 10
Of preliminaries to the election of the Master

So that the election of the Master may be uncorrupt and lawful, as we entirely desire, we therefore will that the Fellows to whom belongs the right of making the election shall before they come to elect the Master have a most sincere regard to three matters. First, that they bring with them a free and sincere conscience, not hampered by favour or any other affection so as to hinder their electing him who shall be plainly deemed in the judgment of all good men to be most worthy; in which matter we require of them all care and faithfulness that may possibly be conceived. Next, that they in no wise promise their votes to any man, nor make any compact, whether open or in secret; but reserve full freedom of judgment until the time of the election. Finally, since we grant to each and all power to nominate those whom they shall know to be worthy of the Mastership (provided that they shall do so three days before the election), that they shall always nominate such a man as is endowed with those gifts which are required under the foregoing statute. And if any shall do the contrary, or nominate someone unworthy, that is, a man not so endowed, he shall at the discretion of the majority of the Fellows be deprived for the space of one whole year of his stipend and other emoluments of his Fellowship, except for his weekly commons. And if anyone shall give his vote for money, whether in the election of the Master or in any other transaction taking place in the name of the College, we desire that he be *ipso facto* removed from the College. And that the Fellows may the more freely cast their votes in the election of the Master, we desire and decree that, if any letter or message on behalf or in favour of anyone shall be sent or addressed by any person to the Fellows, or if a petition from anyone shall be put in, then that person shall be reckoned absolutely to be disqualified for the office of Master, and the election shall *ipso facto* be forthwith held null and void.

NOTES TO CHAPTER 10

Though this has the same title as Christ's XII, the content is quite different. The Emmanuel statute is concerned with principles, not with procedure, which is covered in the next chapter.

CHAPTER II
Of the method and form of election of the Master

Now that this body may not for longer than is proper be without its principal member, we desire and decree that during our lifetime that person or persons shall be Master, Fellows and Scholars of the aforesaid College whom we shall designate and admit. But after we shall have departed out of this life, we ordain that election be made according to the following form. First, that one of the Fellows who is by admission senior among them that shall then be in residence, shall call them together and open the proceedings and as soon as he shall have knowledge thereof shall without any delay make known to them the vacancy in the Mastership, and shall openly and carefully inform them of the day and hour of the coming election. But if any of the Fellows shall be absent, their arrival shall be awaited only for the seven days immediately following. And that the vacancy in the Mastership may the more easily come to the notice of those who are absent, a notice concerning the day and hour of the coming election shall continuously during those seven days be posted on the door of the Chapel by the same senior Fellow; nor do we desire that those who are absent be advised by any other means of the coming election.

On the seventh day therefore after the vacancy is known, at five o'clock in the morning of the same day, both the Fellows and all the Scholars and pensioners shall gather together in the aforesaid Chapel, where first the usual prayers shall be offered to God, and then a sermon shall be delivered either by the senior Fellow himself (if he so wishes) or at his bidding by some other of the Fellows then present, provided that he shall be advised of this duty at least five days beforehand. In this sermon he shall exhort the Fellows to elect as Master such a man as our statutes have described and as the position of the College shall seem properly to require. Afterwards the Eucharist, that is the Lord's Supper, shall be celebrated, in which we desire all the Fellows, Scholars, pensioners, and others resident in the College to participate. When all these exercises of piety and religion are ended, by the which the electors may be roused to the more lively and religious performances of their duty, the aforesaid senior Fellow (all others except the Fellows being first excluded) shall read before them all our statutes concerning the qualification of candidates for the Mastership. And when these have been read the Fellow aforesaid shall appoint as his assistants those two

Fellows who are next in seniority, by admission, of those present, and they shall after receiving the individual votes faithfully manage all things pertaining to the completion of the election; and that they may the more faithfully do so, they shall first look upon the most holy Gospels of Christ and lay their hands thereon and so seal their oath in this manner: 'I, A.B., swear by God from my conscience that in this election I have observed and will observe faithfully and fully the statutes which have just been read, and will choose as Master that person whom my conscience shall adjudge to be indicated and clearly described by these statutes which have just been read, setting aside all unlawful affection, fear, hate, love, and the like.' Which same oath all the other Fellows shall make one after another according to the order of their seniority. And this form of oath and no other do we desire always to be observed before the election of a Master.

When this oath has been taken, the senior Fellow aforesaid shall in the presence of the two other Fellows write down his vote with his own hand; and afterwards the other two also shall likewise write down their votes. Finally all the other Fellows present shall in the presence of the three seniors aforesaid quietly set down their votes and shall write them with their own hands. And all shall write in this or a like form:

'Ego N.T. eligo in Magistrum huius Collegii N.N. etc.'

'I, A.B., choose as Master of this College N.N. etc.'

And all the votes so written shall be read clearly and distinctly by the aforesaid senior or another of the three before all the Fellows present, and that person on whom the majority of those present agree shall be held elected without contradiction by anyone. Which election the said senior, before he withdraws, shall be bound to announce in this form: 'I, A.B., senior Fellow of this College, in my own name and in the name of all the Fellows (*or* of the majority of the same) pronounce N.N. elected Master of this College.' But if the majority of the Fellows neither at the first nor the second scrutiny are able to agree upon one person, then one and all of the Fellows present shall delegate their votes to the five senior, or if there be but four Fellows, to the three senior of all the Fellows present; and that person on whom the majority of the same seniors shall agree shall be deemed elected without any doubt or contradiction. But we forbid these seniors, on pain of loss of their Fellowships *ipso facto*, to complete the election in the same place before twelve o'clock of the same day. Which election the aforesaid senior Fellow or (if he be himself elected Master) the one next him in seniority, on pain of perjury manifest and of permanent expulsion from the College, shall be bound to announce, and to admit the person so elected (if he be in the town) or if not, as soon as he may come there; and the said senior shall with all diligence procure his coming thither.

And the Master elect shall take this oath which follows: 'I, A.B., swear by God that I will sincerely embrace the true Christian religion, contrary to Popery and all other heresies; that I will set the authority of Scripture before the judgment of even the best of men; that other matters, which may in no wise be proved from the word of God, I will hold as of men; but I will regard the King's authority as supreme over all men under his rule, and in no wise subject to the jurisdiction of foreign Bishops, Princes, and Powers; that I will refute all opinions that be contrary to the Word of God, and that I will in the cause of religion always set what is true before what is customary, what is written before what is not written. Secondly, I swear by the same God in Christ Jesus, and I faithfully promise, that I will govern this College, of which I am now elected Master, with all care and diligence, and will preserve intact all its goods, lands, tenements, possessions, revenues, liberties, rights, privileges, and all things whether movable or immovable; that I will so far as in me lies keep inviolate all statutes and ordinances of this College which I know to tend to the glory of God and to the honour and profit of the College, and will take care that they are observed by others; and that, putting aside all exception of persons, I will not make any dispensation contrary to the same statutes or any part thereof, nor cause it to be made by others, nor, if such be made, in any way acquiesce therein. All these things I promise to take upon myself (so far as they be not contrary to the statutes of the realm that have been issued or are to be issued), so help me God through Jesus Christ.'

When these things are done, we desire and decree that the aforenamed senior Fellow (to whom the whole administration and care of affairs were entrusted in the time of the vacancy) or, if he be elected, the Fellow next in seniority, shall immediately after this oath hand over to the newly elected Master a true and complete account of all the affairs of the College under his care and administration; that he shall show him everything in the treasury, the book of statutes, the keys of the chests pertaining to his office, all the ornaments, all the documents and muniments whatsoever pertaining to the said College, and shall hand them over to him to be taken care of according to the tenor of our statutes;

and the Master himself shall within four days complete a new inventory of all these things, which when it has been read and approved by all the Fellows shall be laid up in the College treasury.

NOTES TO CHAPTER 11

Appointment of a successor to Chaderton as Master did not become necessary in the Founder's lifetime. The appointment of Fellows was another matter; initially there were only three, but it was the Founder's intention to build the number up as soon as possible to twelve (cf. chapter 39). A number of formal deeds of appointment, signed by him, are preserved in the Archives (E.C.A., Box 1, NOM.1 to 3, appointing as Fellows William Branthwaite, 18 Dec. 1585; William Bright, 1586/7; Richard Rolph, 4 May 1588; and Box 1, NOM.4 to 9, appointing Scholars).

The procedure for election of a new Master was at Christ's detailed in a number of shorter chapters (XII to XVII). The main differences for Emmanuel are that at the Chapel service a sermon of exhortation is prescribed; and that if two scrutinies do not result in an election, the choice lapses to the five senior Fellows (at Christ's, to the Chancellor or Vice-Chancellor with two senior Doctors or Bachelors of Divinity). The Master's oath after election was at Christ's covered by a separate chapter (XIX) as was the handing over to him of the College Statutes, muniments, etc. (Christ's XXI). In the Emmanuel Master's oath all the words before *Secondly* are new, with emphasis on Protestant faith and loyalty to the Crown; in this they follow similar provisions at Trinity College.

Of inventories of College chattels preserved in the College Archives the earliest, dated 1589, has been published in *ECM*, XLII (1959–60), 35ff. It covers virtually all movables in the Chapel, Hall, Parlour, kitchen, and buttery. (There is a separate inventory of the Library, probably made rather later.) Fresh inventories were made, as here prescribed, after each magisterial election (E.C.A., BUR.8.1).

CHAPTER 12
Of things following the election

When the new Master has been elected and his election announced, the two senior Fellows (all the rest having been by them summoned together) shall communicate the election of the aforesaid Master to the Vice-Chancellor of the University or to his deputy.

NOTES TO CHAPTER 12

The post-election procedure is much simplified from that laid down in Christ's XVIII to XX. There the Master's oath was to be taken, if possible, in the presence of the Chancellor or Vice-Chancellor and the new Master was to enter into formal bonds not to procure dispensation from the Statutes.

CHAPTER 13

Of the removal (if circumstance demand it) of the Master

Care must furthermore be taken not only that some fit person be elected Master, but also that if perchance he go astray he may shortly either reform or be obliged to resign his Mastership. We therefore decree that, if any Master shall be negligent in his administration and in those things which pertain to his office, or shall be gravely suspected of dishonest dealing or of personal misconduct, he shall be once admonished by the Master of Christ's College and the two senior Doctors of Divinity (or failing them the two senior Bachelors of Divinity) in the University; and again a second time, if need be. And if when admonished a second time he amend not himself forthwith; or if he be convicted on certain evidence before the aforesaid Master and the two senior Doctors of Divinity present in the University (or failing them the two senior Bachelors of Divinity) of heresy, of treason, of simony, of usury, of perjury before a justice, of notable theft, of wilful homicide, of manifest incest, adultery, or fornication, of dilapidation or alienation of lands, tenements, or revenues, or of unlawful distraint of goods or property of the College, or of any other comparable offence: then he shall by the aforesaid Master, with the assent of the two Doctors or Bachelors of Divinity, be deprived of the Mastership and all emoluments thereof. We also desire and decree that if it shall happen that the Master be preferred to any ecclesiastical benefice having the cure of souls attached thereto, he vacate *ipso facto* his place in the College aforesaid from the time of his induction to the benefice aforesaid, or of his actual taking possession or receipt of the income thereof; and we give full liberty to the Fellows of the aforesaid College to elect another Master in his place according to the form before prescribed.

NOTES TO CHAPTER 13

This closely follows Christ's xxii; but in the list of possible offences those of dilapidation, alienation, or distraint of College property are new. The provision in the Christ's statute that a Master voluntarily resigning should become a Fellow is omitted. The first Master, Chaderton, did in fact resign in 1622, when over eighty years old, but survived to his 103rd year, dying in 1640. In his retirement he resided at St Nicholas Hostel in St Andrew's Street, and though not a Fellow was often referred to for his knowledge and counsel on College affairs. Under present statutes a retired Master becomes a Life Fellow.

By a College order of 5 August 1628 (E.C.A., COL.14.1) this statute was interpreted to imply that if a beneficed man were elected Master he should relinquish his benefice; but that an 'overlap' period might be allowed, of a duration comparable to that for which a Fellow might retain his Fellowship after induction to a living. On 28 July 1637 (*ibid.*) the interpretation was revised: the statute meant no more than it said; the Master was restrained from taking a benefice after election, but might retain one he already held. William Bennet (in his notes on the Statutes in E.C.A., COL.9.1. vol.II, p. 39) gives a probably apocryphal story that the eighteenth-century Master William Savage temporarily resigned his Mastership in order to accept a living, and retained the living on re-election!

CHAPTER 14

Of the Dean or Catechist

So far we have made statutes concerning the Master; and lest he be
oppressed by too great a burden we set under him a Dean or Catechist,
who shall on the first day of October, or (if that be a Sunday) the second,
be elected by the Master or his deputy and the majority of the Fellows
from among the said Fellows. His duty shall be each year within three
days of the great audit for the whole year to read to all the Fellows and
Scholars then present the Statutes of the College; and every week of
each term within the College Chapel to hear one disputation in Theology, on Friday, for the space of two hours, viz. from four to six,
unless prevented by the celebration of a festival. And he shall be judge
and moderator to set limits to each man's time for stating his thesis, for
objection, and for reply, either more briefly or more at length. We desire
too that he shall note any negligence of his Fellows in celebrating divine
service, approve the cause of their absence or lateness, if it be legitimate, and fine those that are remiss in the same; and that he shall
appoint from among the pupils two monitors who shall write down on
a list the latenesses, absences, and negligence of the other pupils (both
as regards the celebration of divine service and as regards outside
academic exercises), and the Dean himself shall on Friday of every week
have these lists read out. And every week on Saturday at three in the
afternoon for the space of one hour he shall expound and teach some
article of the Christian religion; and at his discretion and judgment shall
examine the Scholars and pensioners and all residing in the College, so
that he may the better know of the progress of each. We also desire that
the rest of the Fellows shall assist him in this examination whenever it
shall be necessary in the judgment of the Master and a majority of the
Fellows. And the Dean shall receive as his stipend fifty-three shillings
and fourpence yearly.

NOTES TO CHAPTER 14

Christ's XXIII provides for *two* Deans, who are referred to as *auxiliaria bracchia*
(auxiliary arms). More significant divergences from the Christ's model are to be
seen in the provisions for religious and academic exercises. While Christ's required
two disputations each week, one in Philosophy and one in Theology, Emmanuel
requires Theology only. St Catharine's (1475) required both; earlier foundations
required disputations also in Laws and Medicine. The Saturday afternoon teaching

and examination of Scholars etc., is new. For further provisions as to academical exercises see chapter 20, with notes.

The Dean's stipend was soon found too slender. By a College order of 25 October 1614 it was agreed he should receive an additional ten pounds a year from study rents.

CHAPTER 15
Of the several fines to be imposed by the Dean

And lest he should punish anyone more severely than is just, we desire
the same [Dean] to observe the following regulations as regards divine
service and theological exercises: first, he shall fine each Fellow, for
each lateness a halfpenny, for each absence one penny, for neglecting
his turn of duty at prayers twelve pence. As to disputations within the
house, the lateness of each Fellow shall be fined a penny, absence four
pence, neglect of his turn six shillings and eightpence. Every pupil, for
lateness at divine service a halfpenny, for absence a penny. At scholastic
exercises, both within the house and outside (as for example the afternoon *sophismata* in the public schools, or the morning sermons *ad
clerum*), for each lateness a farthing, for absence a halfpenny; for neglecting his turn twelve pence, if he be of age; otherwise he shall be corrected
with the rod. By 'lateness' we understand, at disputations, after the
exposition of the respondent's thesis; at divine service, after the first
Psalm. Furthermore, if any of the Fellows does not serve his turn of
duty, then he who is next him in order shall make up for his negligence,
and the delinquent shall nevertheless the next week do him in turn the
same service; and otherwise he shall be fined again. And finally we
desire that the income of these fines shall be devoted towards the
Fellows' victuals. And in levying these fines, as also in repressing the
obstinate arrogance of any persons, if such there be, we command that
the Master be his helper and provide him with that support which it is
proper for the members to receive from the head.

NOTES TO CHAPTER 15

This is essentially the same as Christ's XXIV, except for adjustment of the sums
involved, and redefinition of 'lateness' at divine service. (For Christ's the line was
drawn after the first Psalm at Matins, the first *Kyrie* at Mass and the second Psalm
at Vespers.)

CHAPTER 16
Of the Steward

Next in place after the Dean is the Steward, who shall receive into his hand each month from the Master, Fellows, Scholars, and pensioners, so much money as may suffice for each one's commons; and this shall be regulated by the Master, having in mind what sum is commonly found sufficient per month; and from this money the Steward shall procure such victuals as are necessary to be bought each week. And this shall be set forth, and he shall himself or through the Manciple show in a book to what sum the said commons amount, and the Steward or the Manciple shall give a faithful account every week on Saturday after dinner to the Master or his deputy and the Fellows present. None of the Fellows shall be absent from this audit without the permission of the Master or his deputy, under penalty of two pence.

NOTES TO CHAPTER 16

Christ's xxv, on which this is based, covered both the Steward and the prefect of the common chest, these two officers being described as the 'hands' of the College body. Emmanuel had no keeper of the chest, though mention of him was not eliminated in drafting chapter 6 (q.v.). The requirement that all Fellows attend the weekly audit is new.

CHAPTER 17

Of the qualification of the Fellows

Statutes have so far been made concerning the Master, Dean, and Steward. It remains for us to determine in like manner concerning the Fellows, as being the more important and substantial members of our body. We desire therefore to be elected as Fellows Englishmen, from among the Scholars of the College, who either are Masters of Arts or at least third year Bachelors; and we have determined that at every election those persons be preferred whose patrons are less wealthy, and who are more needy; for which and other reasons moving us, we have determined that those from the counties of Essex and Northampton be preferred before all others, but in such manner that there shall not be more than one from any one county of those aforesaid; which we also desire to be observed in respect of every other county of the whole realm, nor do we permit that there shall ever be more than one Fellow in our aforesaid College from any other county of all England; and as to towns and cities, by whatsoever privileges they may be exempt, we understand them all as pertaining to that county within whose borders they may lie. But if there be found none suitable among the Scholars of the College, it shall be permitted to elect from among others studying within the College, but always from among those that are more needy, of better character, and more learned. We decree moreover that if any be very poor, and have no patrons by whose liberality they may spend their time at the University, at every election these alone be chosen. For it is not just that what we have set apart for the needy alone should ever be diverted to the wealthy or to those who could live comfortably and adequately from other sources without a Fellowship. Such persons therefore we desire not even to be nominated at an election, either by the Master or by any of the Fellows, under penalty of losing a half-year's stipend. These poor men, then, whether they be from the College or from the University, having passed their twenty-first year, we desire to be elected; and we desire them to be skilled, first, in these three tongues, Greek, Latin, and Hebrew, so that they may understand them; next in Rhetoric, Dialectic, and Physic, of which arts they shall both truly know the principles and be able to apply them to use and practice; and above all they shall be professors of pure religion, contrary to Popery and other heresies, and such as have conformed their life and manners thereunto. And since all these qualities may not be suddenly acquired, we desire that no one be admitted a Fellow who shall not have studied in the University of Cambridge for six whole years at the least.

NOTES TO CHAPTER 17

Preference to candidates from certain counties is paralleled at Christ's (chapter XXVI). Essex was the county of the Founder's birth, Northampton of his country residence (Apethorpe, near Oundle) in his maturer years. The rule against more than one Fellow from any single county has its parallel in the choice of Scholars (chapter 32 below).

The exclusion of non-Englishmen (though not mentioned in Christ's XXVII) seems to have been normal in both Oxford and Cambridge. (See J. B. Mullinger, *University of Cambridge*, II, p. 635.)

Preferring the needy candidate was of course no new idea, but there is a fresh emphasis on it here, as on the academic qualifications.

CHAPTER 18
Of preliminaries to election

Now in order that the position and dignities of Fellows of our College
may the more readily be assigned only to men of learning and those
who are endowed with these qualifications, and that those that be
unworthy and bereft of such qualities may always be kept away, we
decree and ordain that, so often as the place of any Fellow shall be
vacant (and we desire that it shall not remain vacant for more than the
space of one month at most), the Master having called together the
Fellows shall advise them five days in advance of the day of the coming
election; in which five days the Master and Fellows ought diligently to
enquire concerning the religion, poverty, learning, and character, of
those who are nominated by them for the coming election. And it shall
be permitted for the Master and each of the Fellows to nominate any
person who shall according to the judgment of their consciences before
God be thought worthy of being chosen at the forthcoming election,
provided that they do so on the fourth day before the election. On
that day we desire that the names of those to be elected be handed in to
the Master on a written paper by each person nominating, so that he
may faithfully keep the names safe in his charge till the day of election.
Therefore any that shall not have been nominated in this manner and
on this day shall not be eligible at that time. And since this matter is of
the greatest importance, we forbid both the Master and the Fellows to
nominate for election any unworthy person, that is, any person who is
not endowed with all the qualifications at least to a moderate degree,
under penalty of loss of a year's stipend, which shall be devoted to the
benefit of the College.

And lest the Master or any of the Fellows should be deceived
through ignorance of the nominees, or through false testimony of others
concerning them, we decree that the Master shall summon the Fellows
to him in some convenient place in the College (as in the Hall or
Chapel, or if occasion demand in his own chamber) in such way that
other students may be present if they wish, and no one in the College be
forbidden to be present; and shall there and in that manner have the
nominees publicly examined for three days before the election. And
first he shall appoint those two Fellows whom he shall judge at that
time most suitable for the office as examiners; and being so appointed
they shall not be bound by any other College exercises during the time

of the election, but shall only prepare themselves to examine and test those nominated; and shall for that purpose be bound for the three days of examination to be present to perform their office. The time of examination shall be from eight o'clock in the morning until ten, unless the Master and a majority of the Fellows shall for just causes decide otherwise to shorten that time, or on account of more necessary College business to transfer it to a time in the afternoon, provided always that at least two hours each day shall be spent in examination. The examiners therefore on the first day shall put the candidates to the test in the Greek and Hebrew languages; and on the second in Rhetoric and Logic; and on the third day in Physic. And on this day also the Catechist, or his deputy, shall on the Master's instruction put them to the test (if need be) in Theology and the true knowledge of God. But we do not desire that the office of examination shall be so restricted to these Fellows that no other may be permitted to act as examiner or opponent; indeed we grant to the Master and any of the Fellows freedom to examine at discretion, provided only that all things be done orderly and seemly. And it is the Master's duty to see that this is religiously observed. And when the examination is finished, and the religion, character, and learning of the candidates are truly known, the Master and Fellows shall prepare themselves for the election in the manner described in the following chapter.

NOTES TO CHAPTER 18

The fullness of this chapter and of the preceding one marks how close they lie to the heart of the Founder's purpose. The Christ's model (xxvii) had spent but one sentence on the examination of candidates.

CHAPTER 19
Of the election of Fellows

Such is the nature of the body politic that, unless new members take
the place of the old, the decay of the whole would gradually ensue;
wherefore we have determined that, so often as any of the Fellows shall
for whatever cause relinquish his Fellowship, a fresh election shall take
place within the four weeks immediately following, unless the situation
of the College shall prevent it on account of some signal loss, in which
case only we permit the election to be deferred until in the judgment of
the Master and a majority of the Fellows the said loss can be fully
repaired. However, we charge the Master and the Fellows on their
consciences to take every care that it be restored as quickly as may be;
and after its restoration they shall without any delay or deferment
proceed to a fresh election, which shall take place in this manner. The
Master and Fellows shall all assemble within the College at a time and
place assigned by the Master; and in their presence the senior Fellow
of those present shall distinctly read out the statutes concerning the
qualifications of Fellows, the preliminaries to election, and the actual
election of Fellows. And in order that the Master and Fellows may the
more freely cast their votes in the election of Fellows or Scholars, we
desire and decree that, if any letter or message on behalf or in favour of
anyone shall be sent or addressed by any person to the Master and
Fellows or to any one of them, then that person shall be reckoned disqualified to hold the place of Fellow or Scholar absolutely, and the
election shall *ipso facto* forthwith be held null and void. We also desire
and decree that none of the Fellows or Scholars aforesaid shall make
any resignation or abdication of his rights except it be unconditional
and absolute. But if anyone shall resign or abdicate his place on condition of the election of a certain person, or on any other condition
whatsoever, we desire that this be regarded as an unconditional resignation, and we determine that his place is vacant from that time, just as
if he had resigned or abdicated unconditionally and absolutely. But
whoever shall give anyone money for his resignation or abdication as
aforesaid, or for his vote, or even shall undertake to give it, shall be
regarded as ineligible, and whoever accepts it shall be duly deprived of
his Fellowship or Scholarship.

Then when the aforesaid statutes have been read, the Master first, and
then the remainder in order of their seniority, shall lay their hands on

the Gospel of Christ and take the following oath. 'I, A.B., call God to witness upon my conscience that in this election I have observed and will observe faithfully and completely the statutes that have just been read, and will elect as Fellow-to-be that person whom in my conscience I judge to be indicated and clearly described by these statutes that have just been read, setting aside all unlawful favour, fear, hatred, love, and such like.' And this same oath shall be taken by all the remaining Fellows, one after the other, observing the order of their seniority. And we desire this form of oath and no other to be observed before the election of Fellows. When this oath has been taken, the Master and the two senior of the Fellows present shall stand in the College Chapel, or in some other place which the Master judges suitable for the purpose, and then the Master and the said seniors shall write their votes with their own hands in this or similar form: 'I, N., elect A.B. a Fellow of this College.' Then each of the Fellows present shall separately write down his vote in the same manner; and that person on whom a majority of the votes of the whole number of the Master and Fellows concur shall be held elected. And we desire it to be understood that in this the Master has one vote only, and that an affirmative vote. And he shall be bound to announce and admit the person so elected. But if the votes of the Master and Fellows be divided in two or more parts so that a majority of those present cannot agree upon one person, then that person on whom the votes of the Master and Fellows together forming a moiety of those present shall agree, shall be held elected without hesitation or contradiction of any kind; and his election shall be announced by the Master in the name of the majority of those present. For in this and similar cases whenever it shall occur in the election of Fellows or Scholars, or in any other appointment, that the Master and Fellows are divided into two equal parts, then we determine that the vote of the Master (whom we permit never to exercise a negative vote) shall be reckoned as two votes for the purpose of the present statute.

The person thus elected shall diligently read through all our statutes which we have set forth for the government of this College, that he may not through ignorance thereof take the name of God in vain; and for this reason he shall be allowed the use of the master copy of the statutes, until he shall have read them through. Then he shall be presented before the society, and shall swear that he will observe all the statutes of this College, according to the following form: 'I, A.B., declare that I will embrace the true religion of Christ, contrary to

Popery and all other heresies, and I promise and bind myself to observe truly and completely each and all of the statutes which Walter Mildmay, founder of this College, has set forth for its government, and I will endeavour as far as in me lies that my co-Fellows shall do the same. I will obey the Master or his deputy in all things soever that he shall lawfully command; I will divulge to no one the secret counsels of the same College (so far as shall be properly permitted); I will hinder nothing by which advantage or honour may accrue to the College, but rather will further it to the best of my ability; I will not consent to any of the Fellows removing to any other faculty than that of Theology to take a degree therein; I will not at any time procure or cause to be procured any dispensation against any of our founder's statutes or against this my oath, nor anyway accept it if procured by another. All these things I take upon myself and by this oath I promise, in so far as they be not repugnant to the statutes of the realm already published or to be published, so help me God through Jesus Christ.' When all these things have been so performed according to our statutes, the Master, after a brief exhortation to the person or persons elected, shall admit them to the society of Fellows in the following form:

'Ego N.N. Magister huius collegii, admitto te in socium eiusdem,

'I, A.B., Master of this College, admit you a Fellow of the same, in nomine Patris et Filii et Spiritus Sancti. Amen.'

in the name of the Father and the Son and the Holy Ghost. Amen.'

NOTES TO CHAPTER 19

This too is much fuller than the corresponding parts of Christ's xxvii, especially in its cautions against favouritism and corruption. The weighting of the Master's vote in case of a tie ensures that, as in the Mastership election (chapter 11 above), the decision is to be reached without reference to anyone outside the College. The declaration of Protestant faith in the new Fellow's oath similarly has its parallel in chapter 11.

CHAPTER 20
Of the worship of God

There are three things which above all we desire all the Fellows of this College to attend to, to wit the worship of God, the increase of the faith, and probity of morals. As regards the worship of God, we first decree that each day, and especially on Sundays, all the Fellows, Scholars, pensioners, and other residents, shall attend public prayers at suitable times to be appointed by the Master or his deputy; at which we desire the Master himself to be present, if he be not lawfully hindered. And he shall at least at the beginning of each term in person deliver a sermon to the Fellows and Scholars of the same College publicly assembled in the Chapel, and shall also at the same time administer the Holy Eucharist; but we exhort him in the name of the Lord that he do both more frequently.

NOTES TO CHAPTER 20

Attendance at Chapel remained in general obligatory (as at other Cambridge colleges) until after the First World War, though the revised Statutes of 1861 gave the Master and Fellows authority to grant exemption.

The infrequent celebration of Holy Communion here prescribed as a minimum was normal in the English church at the time. A College order of 1588 specifies that the three celebrations should be on the third Sunday in each term. (Cf. F. H. Stubbings, *Emmanuel College Chapel*, 1677–1977, Cambridge, 1977, p. 3.) The 1570 University Statutes also prescribed celebration of the Eucharist in college chapels at the beginning of each term (*Documents*, 1, p. 490).

CHAPTER 21

Of the exercises, studies, and orders of the Fellows

As touching the increase of the faith (to which we have allotted the
second place), we would admonish all those who are to be admitted to
this College, be they Fellows or Scholars or pensioners, that in establish-
ing this College we have set before us this one aim, of rendering as many
persons as possible fit for the sacred ministry of the Word and the
sacraments; so that from this seminary the Church of England might
have men whom it may call forth to instruct the people and undertake
the duty of pastors (a matter of all things most necessary). Be it known
therefore to any Fellows or Scholars who intrude themselves into the
College for any other purpose than to devote themselves to sacred
Theology and in due time to labour in preaching the Word, that they
render our hope vain, and hold the place of Fellow or Scholar contrary
to our institution; and we solemnly admonish them diligently to look
to this matter, as they must know that they shall one day give account
to God of the deceit they have committed. And lest we should charge
the whole burden of this duty upon their own unaided consciences,
although we desire them to be learned in Philosophy and the other arts,
and wish the custom of the University to be retained in this, both in
the hearing of lectures and in other exercises, as also in proceeding to
those degrees which are proper in the arts, yet we decree that the Fellows
of the aforesaid College shall every week hold one disputation in
sacred Theology, in which each in his turn shall be respondent; and
there shall be two opponents, which place shall be filled by each Fellow
in turn, according to the custom usual in the other Colleges. And since
we find nothing can be generally prescribed concerning this whole kind
of scholastic exercise in sacred Theology which will fully satisfy our
intentions, or will not run into some difficulty, therefore we give the
Master of the aforesaid College full power, with the consent of a
majority of the Fellows, to prescribe from time to time such more
fruitful manner of exercises as they shall decide to be most convenient
for the promotion of the study of Theology and for the training up of
ministers of the Word. And what is so prescribed we desire to be
observed by all the Fellows, under such penalty as has been appointed
in respect of other exercises. And of the whole number of Fellows of
the said College we desire that at least the four most senior be ministers
of the Word and the sacraments, and that they be admitted to that order

within one year of the date of publication of our statutes in the College aforesaid. And when any of these ministers shall depart from the College, we desire the next of the Fellows in order of his seniority within six months of the retirement of the said minister from the College to be promoted to the order of minister of the Word and sacraments, so that there shall always be in the aforesaid College not fewer than four ministers. And any one who shall not become a minister of the Word and sacraments in accordance with this regulation shall for ever lose the rights of his Fellowship. And those who shall be called to this order of the sacred ministry are to know that we have placed the fullest confidence in their wisdom and diligence, more than in the others, that the rest may be imbued and trained in Christ with the best possible instruction; and we pray them in the Lord that they will make it their duty to be diligently watchful as over a flock that is entrusted to them.

At table at every meal all shall diligently and attentively hear the Bible before and after dinner and supper, until the Master or his deputy shall tell the Bibler to end. Concerning the retention of Latin speech in private and familiar intercourse, we leave it to the judgment of the Master to prescribe what he think fit in that matter, provided that they all make use thereof in such manner as the Master himself shall judge will be useful to them.

NOTES TO CHAPTER 21

Here, as in the preface, we seem to have the Founder himself speaking, re-emphasising the central function of the College. At Christ's (chapter xxx), as also at Trinity (cf. Mullinger, *University of Cambridge*, II, p. 616), a weekly disputation in Philosophy was also laid down. Here Theology reigns supreme. Moreover the Emmanuel statute implies a dissatisfaction with the traditional scholastic disputations, which for the Puritans perhaps smacked too much of pre-Reformation ways of thought. What 'more fruitful manner of exercises' the Master and Fellows did prescribe under this statute may be seen in the College orders: see pp. 99 ff. below. The insistence that the four senior Fellows should be ordained priests makes clear that the Founder intended any reforming trends to be contained within the framework of the established church.

The final paragraph follows Christ's xxx, though that had mentioned the Fathers as an alternative to the Bible for dinner-time readings. The wording of the reference to Latin shows how the drafters were thinking in terms of what to *retain* from earlier practice. At Christ's Statute IV had made it a specific duty of the Master to see that Fellows always spoke Latin in public; at Emmanuel some relaxation was obviously envisaged. Richard Kidder (matriculated 1649) states in his autobiography (ed. A. E. Robinson, *Somerset Record Society Publications*, XXXVII, 1924) that in his day the young scholars were kept to speaking Latin in Hall. The only modern survivals of spoken Latin in the College are for the admission of the Master, Fellows, and Scholars, and in saying grace before and after dinner.

CHAPTER 22
Of vicious manners forbidden to every Fellow

But since it is of little profit that men be learned unless they be good
also, we therefore desire and decree that none of the same Fellows shall
frequent public taverns, houses of ill fame, or any improper place. None
shall engage in drinking parties and carousals or the bearing of arms;
none shall hold secret converse with a woman anywhere, especially in
any of the rooms of the said College, which we desire no woman ever
to enter, if she be alone, nor to remain in the same, except in time of
sickness, in a manner known and approved of the Master or his deputy.
Moreover let none be a walker by night, nor sleep abroad at night
outside the said College at any place within three miles of the same
College, nor venture at all outside the precincts of the College after
nine o'clock on any night from Michaelmas to Easter, or ten o'clock
from Easter to Michaelmas, except for some necessary cause to be
approved by the Master or his deputy. Also none shall keep dogs or
birds of prey, nor play at knucklebones, dice, or cards, even for
recreation. Finally none shall show disrespect to his senior; but shall
give precedence to him both at home and abroad, in Chapel and at
table, in the schools and in the streets, unless perchance he be above
him by reason of some academic degree; for, except his degree prevent
it, we desire that the senior shall always go before the junior in all
places.

NOTES TO CHAPTER 22

This is virtually identical with Christ's xxxi.

CHAPTER 23
Of the stipend and emoluments of the Fellows

And since good men deserve well, and are worthy of reward, we therefore desire and decree that each of the aforesaid ministers shall each year at the customary times receive as his stipend thirty shillings, to be paid in full by the hand of the Master or his deputy. We desire moreover that each week two shillings be paid to the Steward for each Fellow's commons, which sum, if possible, their commons shall not exceed. But if they do sometimes exceed it, each one shall pay the remainder out of his own money, and shall receive the balance if at any time they are less. For clothes each year he shall have twenty-six shillings and eightpence. The expense of bread and wine and other things necessary for the celebration of the Eucharist and public prayers he shall pay out of the common treasury of the College; but if anyone of the Fellows be not a minister, we desire him to be content with the commons and clothing aforesaid, and not to receive anything further of those above mentioned, until he be admitted to the sacred ministry.

NOTES TO CHAPTER 23

It is interesting to compare the actual sums mentioned with those in Christ's XXXII, seventy-eight years earlier. There the payment to a Fellow had been 13s.4d. per quarter (or, if a D.D. or B.D., 16s.8d. or 15s. respectively), as against the mere 7s.6d. at Emmanuel. The difference is seen to be even more disadvantageous when we observe that the Emmanuel payments for commons and clothing (which presumably reflect the rise in actual *costs*) are twice those prescribed for Christ's.

At Christ's the clothing allowance was to be spent at Stourbridge Fair on cloth of a single colour 'so that all may go attired alike when the honour of the College demands it'. At Emmanuel uniformity of colour is prescribed only for the Scholars (see chapter 36 below).

CHAPTER 24
How much they may receive from other sources

If any of the Fellows shall obtain an annual income from which he may conveniently maintain himself, it is not just that he should take the stipends appointed for poor and needy men; therefore we desire and decree that if any of the Fellows shall obtain a patrimony, free chapel, pension, or benefice simple, which exceeds the annual value of ten pounds, then as soon as he shall have the undisturbed possession of any of the same, he shall *ipso facto* cease to be accounted a Fellow. If any of the Fellows of the aforesaid College shall be admitted and instituted to a benefice of whatever value having the cure of souls associated therewith, then as soon as he shall have been inducted to the possession of the same benefice, and shall have obtained the undisturbed possession thereof, or if he shall of his own accord have prevented his induction or undisturbed possession, we desire that his place in the College *ipso facto* become vacant, so that thenceforth he be in no wise accounted or held to be a Fellow of the same College.

NOTES TO CHAPTER 24

At Christ's (xxxiii) the Fellows were allowed to receive benefice income up to ten marks (£6.13s.4d.), but beyond that to forfeit their Fellowship *stipend*. At Emmanuel they are to relinquish the whole status of Fellow. The reasons for the difference are clear: at Christ's it was a prime consideration that Fellows be maintained to say Masses for the Foundress; at Emmanuel the cure of souls in *this* world was the overriding purpose.

free chapel: a chaplaincy without cure of souls.

CHAPTER 25
Of the place of dining and supping

And since we desire them all to be united in one whole, that they may be as it were one body under the Master, the head of the whole College, therefore we desire all the Fellows, the Scholars, and the pensioners of the aforesaid College to dine and sup in the common Hall thereof; and we permit none of them to have dinner or supper apart in their chambers or other places within the College, except for reasonable cause to be approved at the discretion of the Master or his deputy. And although we have decreed that no absent Fellow shall have his commons elsewhere, nevertheless we desire that, if plague or any contagious infection shall arise within the College, or within the Parish in which the said College is situated, or elsewhere within the University of Cambridge, so that a great and notable number of the scholars shall have departed thence on account of the same contagion, then it shall be permitted for the Master and Fellows to betake them to some other place where they may more conveniently be provided for at the same costs as they would have incurred at home. We desire also that if any of them be sick, or be seriously suspected of infection by the plague, so that he shall be unable conveniently to go among them that are well, and if it be so agreed by the Master and a majority of the Fellows, then by their permission he shall find himself some suitable place where he may dine, and receive the aforesaid emoluments, to wit for stipend, commons, and clothing, just as if he were present in College.

NOTES TO CHAPTER 25

This reproduces Christ's xxxiv. For details about meals see the College orders of 1588 (below).

Plague was of course a real risk in the sixteenth and seventeenth centuries, and this statute was invoked for closures of the College in 1630 and 1638, as well as during the great epidemic of 1665.

CHAPTER 26
How long the Fellows shall be permitted
to be absent from the said College

Every man is sometimes pressed by business, so that it may sometimes
be necessary to travel some distance from the College; and for this
reason we decree that in each year every Fellow shall have at discretion
twenty days holiday, during which he may be absent from the said
College, provided that he shall have asked permission beforehand of
the Master or his deputy, and with due respect. And if his cause be so
urgent that the Master or his deputy shall in his conscience and before
God approve it as necessary, then we desire that he may be able to
grant thirty days more within the same year, either at the same time or
separately. And besides this, if some other cause arise, or the same
become more pressing, and if it shall before God and their consciences
seem just to the said Master or his deputy and a majority of the Fellows,
then by permission of the Master or his deputy the same Fellow may
again absent himself for other thirty days within the same year. But if
anyone shall absent himself longer than these periods and this specified
number of days within the space of one year (unless on account of
serious illness or forceful detention which shall be approved by the
Master and a majority of the Fellows) so that he return not within the
stated number of days, we desire that he forthwith be deprived of all
rights of his Fellowship in the said College. And if any of the Fellows
shall be lawfully absent whose return shall seem to the Master or his
deputy and a majority of the Fellows to be necessary to the advantage
and honour of the College, and if when recalled he return not at once
as soon as he conveniently may, unless he shall state just reason
therefor, to be approved of the same, he shall similarly be deprived of
his Fellowship. We desire the granting of this permission to the
Fellows to be so regulated that not more than one third of the Fellows
be absent at one and the same time. And also throughout all the time
that they are absent (except in the circumstances mentioned in the preceding statute) none of them shall be allotted anything for his commons
from the funds of the College, but the commons of everyone who is
absent shall be paid into the common chest.

NOTES TO CHAPTER 26

Virtually identical with Christ's xxxv. By a College order of 28 July 1637 it was agreed that acceptable reasons for prolonged absence should include legal business requiring personal attendance, the death of a very near friend, and business concerning the acceptance of a living.

CHAPTER 27
Of the office, duties and stipend of the Tutors

Since it is agreed that, in the instruction of youth, the greatest value
resides in the care and diligence of tutors, we therefore desire each of
the Scholars and pensioners of the aforesaid College to have a Tutor,
who shall be responsible for their morals and diligence, and, when need
be, diligently instruct them, and especially train them up in pure
religion and the true knowledge of God. And we do not permit the
Tutors who undertake this charge to be anyone other than the Master
and Fellows. And lest the Scholars or pensioners or sizars be over-
burdened by this office, we desire that the Scholars and sizars aforesaid
shall pay nothing whatever to their Tutors by way of annual salary or
fees; also that pensioners admitted to the table and society of the
Fellows shall not be obliged to pay more than forty shillings a year,
and other pensioners not more than twenty-six shillings and eightpence,
by way of annual fees and salary. If any of the Tutors shall receive or
demand under this head more than has been prescribed, then, unless
when admonished by the Master he shall abstain from such demands, he
shall in no wise be admitted to hold the office of Tutor, and the Master
shall assign those entrusted to his care to some other Tutor or Tutors
for instruction. And lest anyone should take under his tutorship more
pupils than is expedient, we entrust the regulation of their number to
the Master. So therefore none of the Fellows shall take anyone under
his tutorship except with the consent of the Master, nor shall he retain
a greater number than the same shall think expedient. We desire that
each of the aforesaid Tutors, if he have two or more pupils committed
to his tutorship, shall have at least two of them sleeping in his chamber,
unless the Master shall see good cause why this number should be
decreased. And those who are under the charge of Tutors shall never
go out into the town without their Tutors' consent, except to hear
lectures in the public schools, or when other academic exercises or
public meetings are to be held, or when public gatherings in the
University are announced.

NOTES TO CHAPTER 27

This statute is entirely new, though the tutorial system was already in existence at
other colleges, even if not by statute. It should be noted however that the Tutor–
pupil relationship was still much more a matter of personal choice and arrangement
than nowadays.

CHAPTER 28
*Of the visitation of students' rooms,
so that idle gatherings be not held therein*

Among the many undesirable things that hinder the progress of them
that be studious of good learning, no little harm is done by the frequent
converse of the young upon idle matters; for besides the waste of time
(which is to be accounted not among the least of the damages) there is
engendered in youthful minds an evil habit by which they are most
easily diverted from serious things to frivolities and foolishness. We
therefore decree and ordain that neither pensioners nor Scholars nor
sizars nor subsizars (unless they be Masters of Arts) shall presume to
hold any meetings in their chambers either for play, for feasting, for
conversation, or under any other pretext whatsoever. And whosoever
shall act contrary to this rule, if he be of age, shall be fined twelve pence
for each occasion by the Master or, in his absence, his deputy; or if he
be not yet out of the age of boyhood, he shall be punished by the Dean
by beating. And that this may be more strictly observed, we decree and
ordain that the Fellows, one or two at a time, at the discretion of the
Master, shall each in their turn inspect and visit the chambers of such
pensioners, Scholars, sizars, and subsizars, at night, at least twice each
week; and they shall diligently discover what is passing in each, and
shall commend the diligent and reprove the negligent; and whomsoever
they find violating this statute, they shall the next day report their
names so that they may be fined as above ordained. And the fines in
money from offenders of this sort shall be devoted towards the Fellows'
victuals.

NOTES TO CHAPTER 28

This too is new.

As is well known, undergraduates sometimes came into residence as young as
fourteen; and corporal punishment was a recognised feature of the training of
children.

sizars and sub-sizars: The number of these is not defined in the Statutes, unless
they are to be identified with the ten poor men referred to in chapter 39 below.
Sizars were poor students, not on the foundation, who partly paid their way by
undertaking domestic chores or personal service to a Fellow or Fellow-Commoner
as mentioned in chapter 40 below. In more recent times the title of sizar has been
applied to undergraduates of limited means awarded a small money grant from the
Scholarships Fund. The word is apparently derived from *size* in the sense of a
portion of bread and drink; the sizar presumably had his *sizes* free. The eighteenth-
century College historian William Bennet tells us that the sizars' high-table waiting
duties were finally abolished in 1770 (E.C.A., COL.9.1B. p. 31).

CHAPTER 29
Of the Lecturer and Sub-Lecturers

We observe that this body still lacks one most necessary member, by means of which new offspring may be engendered. We desire therefore and decree that some one of their number shall be elected by the Master and a majority of the Fellows as College Lecturer. No one who is elected shall refuse this office, under pain of loss of his Fellowship, but he shall be bound diligently to exercise it so long as the Master and a majority of the Fellows think it to the advantage of the College. On weekdays, according to the custom of the University observed in other colleges, the bell having first been rung immediately after morning prayers, the Lecturer himself shall hear the lecturers [sic] reading publicly in the Hall of the College for the space of one hour; he shall examine their classes as often as shall be necessary, and shall diligently see to it that these are examined by his Sub-Lecturers. What books are to be studied in each class, and in what manner they are to be expounded, we leave to the judgment of the Master and Dean. But if the Lecturer himself desire to expound some book (and this we enjoin him from time to time to do), he shall choose what book he likes from the works of Plato, Aristotle, or Cicero. The Master and a majority of the Fellows shall decide at their discretion at what hour, for how long, and at what times of the year he is to lecture. He shall moreover be present and act as Moderator at the scholastic disputations and at all exercises from beginning to end, according as shall be laid down by the Master and a majority of the Fellows. And that the Lecturer be not burdened with too great a load, we desire Sub-Lecturers to be chosen by the Master and a majority of the Fellows, either from among the Fellows (if possible) or from among the Masters and Bachelors who are not Fellows. And each of these shall perform his duty in person, unless he be prevented by some legitimate cause to be approved by the Master, when we desire him to substitute at his own costs some other suitable man who in the Master's judgment will diligently fill his place.

NOTES TO CHAPTER 29

This, including the physiological metaphor, follows Christ's xxxvi. There the lecture subjects were more particularly defined: each day there was to be one in *Sophistria* (i.e., Dialectic), one in Logic, one in Philosophy, and one on the poets or orators. The Christ's statute made no provision for Sub-Lecturers.

In the third sentence 'hear the lecturers' must refer to *Sub*-Lecturers though the MSS read *lectores*.

On the books prescribed for study see the 1588 orders (below) under *Bookes for lectures*, p. 101.

CHAPTER 30
Of the stipend of the Lecturers

But since it is just that all work be compensated by its reward, we desire and decree that in each quarter thirteen shillings and fourpence be paid to the Lecturer as stipend by the Master or his deputy in addition to the other emoluments to be assigned to him by the Master and a majority of the Fellows. And we therefore desire and decree that in each of the matters aforesaid every one shall carry out his duties in his own person, unless he shall be prevented by legitimate cause approved by the Master, when he shall at his own costs substitute some other of the Fellows, fitted to perform this duty, who will in the Master's judgment diligently fill his place. But if he shall be involved in any business which demands his prolonged absence, or if he be afflicted by serious and prolonged illness, or if he shall have obtained some promotion by reason of which he must relinquish the rights of his Fellowship, then we desire the office to be committed by the Master and a majority of the Fellows to some other of their number. The Sub-Lecturers' stipends shall at the discretion of the Master and a majority of the Fellows be deducted from the Lecturer's stipend, and shall be paid to them individually by the Master or his deputy.

CHAPTER 31

Of the authority of the Lecturer over his pupils

But this member will be useless unless it have seed whence new progeny may be born and produced. We therefore desire and decree that all Scholars of this College, and likewise the pensioners resident therein, and any others whom the Master and a majority of the Fellows shall deem necessary, shall apply themselves diligently to the lectures and other scholastic exercises aforesaid. And the Lecturer shall at his discretion punish and fine them if they come later than they should to the lectures or other scholastic exercises, or if they shall be absent from the same, or though present not attend diligently: for lateness (that is, if they are not present for the beginning of any lecture, sophism, problem, opponency, examination, or disputation) – one farthing; if they are absent for more than half of any one of these – one halfpenny; if for the whole, we desire each pupil to be fined one penny; and so for each occasion that they offend in any of the aforesaid, if they be of age; otherwise they shall be punished with the rod. And the income from these fines we assign to the Fellows' victuals. But if the Lecturer shall show himself too harsh and severe to anyone, he shall be corrected at the discretion of the Master and the senior Fellow. And if any pupil after frequent punishment will not amend himself, the Lecturer himself shall refer the matter to the Master and a majority of the Fellows; and if after being admonished by them three times he persist in notable negligence, we desire him to be deprived of all his privileges in the aforesaid College and to be permanently excluded from it.

NOTES TO CHAPTERS 30 AND 31

These are essentially the same as Christ's xxxvii and xxxviii; but there the fines went to the Lecturer himself 'that he may pay more diligent heed to his office'.

CHAPTER 32

Of the qualification and election of the Scholars

Lest, therefore, this seminary be unfit and unruly, and incapable of
gentle and seemly governance, we desire and decree that the Scholars
shall be chosen from among such young men as are distinguished by
poverty, honesty, and outstanding capacities, persons of proved ability
and good promise, not Bachelors of Arts nor yet admitted to the sacred
ministry, but who intend to take up Theology and the sacred ministry;
and they shall be at least moderately instructed and skilled in Greek,
Rhetoric, and Logic. Those that are poor shall be preferred, provided
that they be equal in other qualifications. Wherefore we especially
desire to give preference to those born in the counties of Essex or of
Northampton; from which we desire that there shall always be two
Scholars in the same College; provided that there shall not at any one
time be more than three Scholars from either of these counties, nor
from any other county in all England. And we desire the same form to
be observed in the election and examination of Scholars as we have
described in the statutes of the election of Fellows and of the preliminaries thereto.

NOTES TO CHAPTER 32

This differs little from Christ's xxxix, apart from a requirement there that candidates
be able to speak and understand Latin, and in the list of preferred counties. In the
first sentence all MSS read *probitate, indole, ac bona spe*, which is not properly trans-
latable. There has probably been an accidental corruption of *probate indolis ac bone
spei* (Christ's xxxix).

On the limitation to three from any one county cf. chapter 17. From the earliest
years of the College every man's county of birth has been recorded on admission –
a practice still maintained.

CHAPTER 33
Of the oath of the Scholars

And since the violation of a sacred oath is a thing for all men most greatly to be feared, we therefore desire and decree that each one of the Scholars, soon after his election and before he is admitted to enjoy any emolument within the said College, shall in the presence of the Master and a majority of the Fellows lay his hand upon the most holy Gospels of God and swear on oath in the following form: 'I, A.B., call God to witness, that I will wholly and in truth observe each and all of the statutes which Walter Mildmay, founder of this College, enacted for the administration of the same, to the best of my power, and so far as they concern me, and I will endeavour that others do the same. I will obey the Master or his deputy in all things that he shall lawfully command; I will keep secret the counsels of the College, if I hear any that ought not to be published; I will show due honour and respect to each and all of the Fellows; and I will attempt nothing which I believe may be turned to the detriment or dishonour of the Master, or of any of the Fellows, or of the College itself; neither will I, so long as I shall live, in any way consent with those who do so. All these things I take upon me, so far as they be not repugnant to the statutes of the realm already enacted or to be enacted; and so I promise by this oath, so help me God through Christ Jesus.'

NOTES TO CHAPTER 33

This is little changed from Christs XL, apart from omission of a final provision that a copy of the College Statutes be kept chained to a stall in the Chapel for the information of Scholars. Nowadays all Scholars are provided with a printed copy of such statutes as concern them. They are still required to read a declaration (no longer in the form of a religious oath), in the presence of the Master and Fellows, promising obedience to the Statutes.

CHAPTER 34
*Of divine service, of academic exercises,
and of the manners of the pupils*

There is nothing a young man should shun so much as idleness and inaction; and therefore we desire and decree that every pupil be always occupied, so far as may be, either in the worship of God, or in the study of good learning, or in the cultivation of distinguished manners. On all Sundays and other days of public prayer without exception we desire them to be present throughout at each of the divine offices in the Chapel of the said College. Each one shall also attend at all lectures and other academic exercises whatsoever, both within the College and without, in the public schools, according to his years and capacity, and according to the custom of the University; and shall proceed to his degrees at such time as he properly and worthily can, and indeed as soon as the University's own statutes allow. Moreover we desire the Fellows and Scholars aforesaid to conduct themselves decently and respectably both at home and abroad; to refrain from quarrelling and fighting; to be frequent in their attendance at public sermons; to show modesty in countenance, in deportment, and in the form and fashion of their apparel; to apply themselves diligently to study, so that they may show forth their diligence by the very fruits thereof. And if in the aforementioned matter anyone shall not meet with the Master's approval, then we desire him to be admonished by the Master with the assistance of the Dean to amend his manners, or the form and fashion, or the neglect, of his apparel; and if he shall not so rectify himself that his amendment may be apparent to the Master, we desire that he be deprived of his commons, until he have rectified himself; and if, when admonished a second and third time according to the aforesaid form, he shall not obey, or shall not in the Master's judgment satisfactorily amend his faults or negligences, then he shall be brought to have his case tried before the Master and Fellows in the College, and if the Master and a majority of the Fellows so decide we desire that he be deprived for ever of his rights as a Fellow or Scholar or pensioner, without any further appeal or complaint.

NOTES TO CHAPTER 34

In this statute *days of public prayer* replaces the pre-Reformation *feast-days* of Christ's
XLI. It is worth noting that *superpelliciis candidis induti*, 'dressed in white surplices',

is omitted. Surplices were still normal in other College chapels, and in the early seventeenth century their disuse was remarked on as typical of Emmanuel's nonconformity (cf. Stubbings, *Emmanuel College Chapel*, p. 3).

The provisions about deportment, dress and discipline are new, and although much the same would probably have been officially expected of young students in other colleges, it seems intended that Emmanuel should be distinctive. Richard Kidder (cf. note on chapter 21) states that in his day (*c.* 1650) the College was 'a Schoole of Vertue as well as learning', in which the Fellows 'watched over the young students with that care, and inspected their studies with that diligence that it was not easy for them to miscarry'. Admonition for ill behaviour was a serious matter, recorded in a book which still survives (E.C.A., CHA.1.4.¹). In Chaderton's Mastership there were forty-four admonitions, a little over one a year. Offences in that time include disobedience, neglect of Chapel services or studies, quarrelling and fighting, drunkenness, climbing in after hours, and being 'taken by the Proctor in a scandalous house'.

CHAPTER 35
Of the duties to be performed within the College

And lest perchance the Scholars be hindered from learning by duties towards the Master and Fellows, we desire and decree that neither the Master nor any of the Fellows shall press any of the Scholars to perform any duties for them, nor to undertake any business for the College, except at dinner, supper, and bevers in the Hall of the same College, or at the times of divine service in the Chapel, on which occasions we desire six of them each week (or more or less at the Master's discretion) to take each their turn of duty in serving at the Fellows' table, carefully carrying in and out such things as pertain thereto, and in reading the Bible before and after dinner and supper. But at other times let them apply themselves to their education and good learning, whereby they may proceed to their academic degrees as soon as the proper time comes. For we desire that no one be retained in the said College as a Scholar after he has once attained such years' standing as will permit him to take the degree of Master of Arts. But if the Master and a majority of the Fellows shall think fit that the duties aforesaid, or any of them, be performed by others than Scholars of the said College, we decree that they may commit and assign the said duties to others at such times and to such persons as seems best.

NOTES TO CHAPTER 35

Although the corresponding Christ's XLII prescribed more particular duties for the Scholars in Chapel, the content and emphasis of this statute is otherwise little changed.

bevers: a word used for any 'sup and bite' between principal meals. On the times of meals in the early days of the College see the 1588 orders (below).

Nowadays the Scholars read grace before dinner in Hall; and until the 1930s they read the lessons at the daily services in Chapel. According to William Bennet (commenting on this statute in E.C.A., COL.9.1. vol.II) the duty of waiting at high-table was very soon transferred to the sizars; and even that custom had ceased in Emmanuel, as in most colleges, by 1770.

CHAPTER 36
*How much the Scholars shall receive from the College,
and how much from others, and of their absence*

And that the Scholars may have a keener incitement to study we desire
and decree that each week there be credited to the Steward for commons
for each one of them twelve pence, which sum they shall receive from
the said College at the two customary times of year; and so far as may
be possible we do not wish their commons to exceed that sum; but if
they shall exceed that sum, then the individual Scholars shall be required
to pay the balance to the Steward from their own money, and when
their commons are less shall receive any surplus back again. And for
their year's clothing, fourteen shillings and eight pence; for which
clothing we desire the Master to assign a set colour. Further we desire
them all to sit together at dinner and supper in the Hall of the College
at the tables appointed for them; four of them to sleep in each chamber,
and not more. And if any of them shall be presented with any property
from which he receive annual income above the value of eight marks, or
with any benefice having the cure of souls attached thereto, we desire
that upon receiving undisputed possession of the same he relinquish
each of his emoluments. And finally that no one of them may be absent
from the same College for a whole day or night without the permission
of the Master or his deputy, nor be absent for more than twenty days
in one year, unless the Master or his deputy and a majority of the
Fellows shall have agreed that he has just and necessary cause; and for
the time of his absence no allowance shall be made to anyone, as we
have before decreed concerning the Fellows.

NOTES TO CHAPTER 36

The Scholars at Christ's (chapter XLIII) received no statutory clothing allowance,
though the Fellows did (cf. chapter 23 above). Like the latter they had the free
services of a College barber and launderer, omitted at Emmanuel.

The continuity of residence through the year is notably in contrast with modern
practice. Although the students did not go home, most colleges had a holiday period
over Christmas, when College plays and other diversions were permitted. There is
no record of such frivolity at Emmanuel. By a College order of 1598 the permitted
period of absence was increased to nine weeks a year.

CHAPTER 37
Of the Manciple, the cooks, the
launderer, and a servant for the Master

Lastly, we note within the said College, certain persons below the pupils themselves, to wit servants and hirelings, who we consider should be regarded as the feet for the whole body; and it will not be superfluous to make some ordinance about them.

In the first place, we desire that there be a Manciple, who at the discretion of the Steward shall provide the bread, drink and victuals necessary for the said body, and who shall hold the keys of the pantry and buttery, to minister to each when need shall arise. He shall hold a reckoning each week with the bakers and brewers; and he shall also in consultation with the Steward make up the books at the end of each week for the commons account; and finally he shall hand over to the Master or his deputy the keys of all the gates of the College, both front and back, after the same have been locked at night at the proper hour. Moreover, that he may the more diligently perform all this, we desire him to receive as wages each quarter six shillings and eight pence besides Scholar's commons, and the reasonable profits, not a few, which will arise from his reckonings with the baker, the brewers and the butchers, unless the Master for just cause shall decide that some part should be subtracted from the aforesaid profits to be applied to the uses of the College. There shall be also one head cook for the preparation of food, who besides the business of cooking shall assist the Manciple in the purchase of victuals, and who shall receive as wages each quarter six shillings and eightpence besides Scholar's commons and the cook's profits belonging to him. There shall be set below him an under-cook, who shall serve under him, and shall clean the several cooking vessels; whose wages shall be, for commons twelve pence each week, and such other kitchen profits as are allowed to the under-cook at Christ's College. Nor is it less necessary that all the linen cloths of the College which it is necessary to use on the tables be washed each week; therefore we desire that some man fitted for this task be provided, of good and honest conversation; who shall receive for wages every quarter six shillings and eightpence; and we desire that no one of the above-mentioned paid servants be hired without the consent of the Master and a majority of the Fellows; and we allow besides these someone as man-servant for the Master for his private business, whose wages we have appointed before.

NOTES TO CHAPTER 37

The equivalent statute at Christ's (XLIV) includes among the domestic staff a College barber to keep the Master, Fellows, and Scholars, in weekly trim. At Emmanuel this was presumably left to personal initiative, as was the laundering of clothes (cf. chapters 36 and 23 above). As the Emmanuel launderer had only table linen to wash, his wages are but half those of his Christ's counterpart (who, incidentally, might be a woman). Tablecloths for the Hall appear in the earliest College inventories, and were usual until the present century. It is related that when they were first dispensed with the then senior Fellow used to re-lay his knife and fork etc., on his napkin and ask for another (which the waiter did not provide until asked for).

On the *Steward* see chapter 16 above. The *Manciple* was equivalent to the modern catering manager.

The Master's man-servant's wages were to be 26s.8d. a year (chapter 7).

CHAPTER 38
Of presentations to vacant livings

A great burden of responsibility is laid upon us by those who, relying on the good faith and judgment of the Master and Fellows, have entrusted, or intend to entrust to this our College, those churches of which they are themselves patrons, so that they may be committed to the best pastors that may be. Wherefore, in order that their pious desires and opinions may be satisfied, and in the interest of those persons the well-being of whose souls assuredly depends to no small extent upon the pious ordering of those churches, we exhort the Master and Fellows in the Lord, that, in appointing pastors to these churches, and to those of which hereafter the care may in the same manner be given up to them by the patrons thereof, they act in sincerity, and neither regard any man's favour in that matter, nor be moved by gifts, but cast their votes for that man whom, their own conscience guiding them, they shall esteem to be best endowed with those gifts which the Holy Spirit bestows upon the true pastor, being resolved that, if any sin be therein knowingly committed by them, they must hereafter render account thereof before the Supreme Judge, as for the betrayal of a brother's blood. And that this whole business of electing pastors may be the more carefully administered, we desire and decree, that within the space of three months from the time when they shall know that a pastor is wanting in some one of the said churches (whether this shall have come about by the death of him who last held that office, or by deprivation or by resignation, or in any other manner) they shall elect one of their own number whom they shall resolve to be most fit, and who shall hold no other ecclesiastical benefice having the cure of souls or the requirement of residence or frequent attendance annexed thereto whether by the laws, statutes or customs of this realm, or under the foundation of the benefice itself, or by local statute; and that they shall effectively present him to the bishop of that diocese in which the living shall be vacant, or to whatever other person shall have the power of instituting the pastor or rector, to be admitted and instituted by the same as pastor or rector of the church aforesaid. But we entirely forbid that persons be chosen for presentation as pastors or rectors of the churches from elsewhere than the College itself, since we have no doubt that it will suffice to supply men fitted for that office.

Moreover we desire and decree that no one be presented to undertake the cure of a vacant church except he have first given suitable surety to the Master and Fellows of the aforesaid College that, so long as he retains the position of pastor or rector of that church to which he is presented, he will diligently reside in the aforesaid church according to the requirement of the common law; neither will he obtain or accept any dispensation which will free him from the requirement of residence; and that so long as he is pastor or rector of that church he will neither accept nor retain any ecclesiastical benefice, dignity, or office, having the cure of souls annexed thereto, or which shall tie him to residence or frequent attendance away from the said church, whether by requirement of the laws or customs of this realm or of the foundation or of local law or custom. Finally, that all base practice may be removed from this business, and all be done piously and religiously as the gravity of the matter itself requires, we desire and decree that, if the Master or any of the Fellows of the aforesaid College shall be convicted of having accepted money or any kind of gift for casting his vote in the presentation of a pastor to any of the aforesaid churches, or for transferring his vote to anyone, he shall for ever lose that position which he holds in the aforesaid College. We wholly preclude from the Master and Fellows all power of delegating advowsons to any person, as also the power of consenting to impropriations.

NOTES TO CHAPTER 38

This chapter is entirely new, and essential to the Founder's purpose. Cf. the note on *advowsons* at chapter 1 above.

CHAPTER 39

Of the augmentation of wages and other allowances to the Master,
Fellows, and Scholars, as to the other officers of the College,
according as income shall increase

Although we have before prescribed the wages of the Master, Fellows,
Scholars and other officers, and how much is to be allotted to each for
daily victuals, yet, since we have been obliged to regulate them in
accordance with the present rate of revenues of the aforesaid College
(though willingly ready to make them more generous, were the said
revenues sufficient), we hope that it will come about that they will
hereafter be so augmented by the generosity of good men that there
may be sufficient wherewithal to make more generous allowance to the
said Master, Fellows, and Scholars, and other officers. We therefore
desire and decree that, if it shall come about that the annual revenues of
the said College shall hereafter be in any manner increased, then the
wages and other allowances made to the Master, Fellows, Scholars, and
other officers, by virtue of our aforesaid ordinances, be augmented in
proportion to the increase of the aforesaid revenues, and having regard
to the standing of each of them; but in such manner that the allowance
to the Master exceed not the sum of forty pounds annually, and that
what shall be appointed for any one of the Fellows exceed not the sum
of ten pounds annually, nor that more be allowed to any Scholar than
the sum of four pounds annually, nor that the wages of any of the aforesaid officers exceed the sum of forty shillings, unless it shall be otherwise
decided by the aforesaid Founder, so long as he shall live. We do not
however desire that the wages or allowances aforesaid be augmented
until the resources of the College be so augmented that they may supply,
besides the Master, twelve Fellows and thirty Scholars, so that they
have the same wages and allowances as the rest, as has been before
prescribed, together with ten poor men who shall serve at the Fellows'
table and shall live upon the remains of that table, and to each of whom
shall also be given from the revenues of our College one groat weekly.
When the number of Scholars shall have reached forty, then the Master
shall receive fifty pounds for his wages and allowances; and if the
aforesaid number of Scholars shall reach fifty, then he shall receive
sixty pounds.

NOTES TO CHAPTER 39

This too is new, though not the principle that all on the foundation must share in the financial fortunes (good or bad) of the College. While Fellows and Scholars alike owed their whole livelihood to the endowment, unassisted by any University stipend or government grant – and for some at least this was true down to the present century – the corporate feeling was likely to remain strong. After the Second World War general economic trends, together with conscious policy as to the relation between Colleges and the University, resulted in a progressive diminution in the value of the Fellow's share in the corporate income of the College, until in 1966 this 'dividend', as it was called, was abolished entirely. At the present time a Fellow is still entitled to significant privileges in kind (such as dinner in Hall) but receives no money from the endowment *as a Fellow* (as distinct from payment for teaching or for fulfilling a particular College office, such as that of Bursar or Tutor or Librarian).

The initial number of Fellows was three; but four more were elected within the first year, and by 1588 there was a full complement of twelve (cf. note on chapter 11 above, and the College orders below).

ten poor men: these are not otherwise specifically referred to; but the description of their status suggests they might be the same as the sizars alluded to in chapters 27 and 28 and again (though not under the name of sizar) in chapter 40, which allows for certain students acting as servants to Fellows or Fellow-Commoners.

CHAPTER 40
Of the admission of pensioners to the College

If we consider thus far whence hurt or ill to this body may arise, we do not see that that may easily occur from the members themselves, since so careful trial is to be made of each person before he be received into that number. What therefore we most fear is the admission of commoners and pensioners beyond that number, whose unwholesome conversation will perchance corrupt the others, and so the decay of the whole of the rest of the body gradually ensue.

We therefore desire and decree that no one else be admitted as a pensioner to share in the life and conversation in the said College, except he be on the testimony of the Master and a majority of the Fellows of honest life and unsullied reputation, and one who shall before the Master and a majority of the Fellows have promised faithfully that he will conform himself to the Scholars, Fellows, or pupils, in the cultivation of honest manners, in the performance of academic exercises, and in the celebration of divine service, and that he will submit to these our statutes and laws, before he be admitted into the said College. Nor do we permit any of the aforesaid pensioners to remain longer in the College than he shall diligently perform the academic exercises and strive to be of such character as shall be approved by the Master's judgment. And we desire no one to be admitted as a pensioner to share the life of the Fellows or Scholars, nor to remain in the College, who has obtained any benefice having the cure of souls annexed thereto, and who has no chamber in which to stay in the said College. Further we desire that no one be admitted to share the board and society of the Fellows except he be a Master of Arts or a Bachelor or Doctor of Divinity, or else the son of a Knight or some other man distinguished by rank of higher nobility, except for some just and fit cause to be approved by the Master and a majority of the Fellows. Moreover we allow none of the Fellows of the said College nor of the pensioners admitted to share the board and society of the Fellows, to be permitted to have a man-servant, unless the servant have a chamber in College and apply himself to learning, to perform all the exercises which shall be prescribed for Scholars and pensioners according to the ability and progress in learning of each. Further we desire the pensioners to sleep four in a room, unless it shall seem right to the Master for just causes to assign one room to two at least. The pensioners admitted to the

society of the Fellows shall pay each quarter two shillings to be applied
to necessary uses at the discretion of the Master and a majority of the
Fellows; and those admitted to the society of the Scholars shall pay
twelve pence each quarter.

NOTES TO CHAPTER 40

The first half of this follows Christ's XLV; but all after the words *and in the celebration
of divine service* is new, including the provisions concerning those admitted 'to share
the board and society of the Fellows', i.e., Fellow-Commoners.

At this point there followed, at Christ's, two statutes (XLVI and XLVII) *of the
visitor* and *of the manner of visitation*. Emmanuel was unusual in having no standing
visitor to whose arbitration difficulties or disputes might be referred, and who might
have the duty (as at Christ's) of an annual inspection. There was provision, however,
as already seen, for reference or appeal to the Vice-Chancellor, with assessors, on
certain matters (see, e.g., chapters 2, 3, above).

CHAPTER 41
Of the interpretation of ambiguities and obscurities

But if any obscurity shall appear in these our statutes which shall require interpretation of necessity, we reserve the interpretation of it to ourselves (so long as we shall live), and we desire that the Master, Fellows and Scholars aforesaid be content therewith, and hold and observe it for ever as a statute of the College. And after God in his mercy shall have called us out of this life, then if any ambiguity or obscurity shall appear thereafter, we desire the Master and those Fellows who are present in the College to discuss it, and to have and to hold as true and legitimate that interpretation which the majority of them shall make. But if there shall not be agreement among those just aforesaid, or if any one of the Fellows or Scholars shall complain that that interpretation is unfair, then within ten days from the time of the aforesaid discussion we desire that an approach be made to the Master of Christ's College and the two senior Doctors of Divinity of the University aforesaid, and whatever opinion of the disputed statute shall be decided upon by two of the same, we desire that the aforesaid dispute be terminated thereby, and that all acquiesce therein.

NOTES TO CHAPTER 41

This runs parallel to Christ's XLVIII in that ambiguities of interpretation are, during his lifetime, to be settled by the Founder himself. Thereafter, however, doubts are to be settled within the Fellowship if possible. Reference to the Master of Christ's (in the capacity of an *ad hoc* visitor) is only a last resort.

CHAPTER 42
Of the common estate of all who shall be in the College

Although we willingly concede to marriage that honour which is accorded to it by the Holy Spirit in Holy Writ, and reject the opinion of those who have held that matrimony ought to be forbidden to a certain order of men, yet there are many and grave causes why we should suffer no one of those who shall be numbered among the members of our College to be married. We therefore desire and decree that if anyone hereafter who has a wife shall be elected in the College aforesaid, his election shall be held void, as of one unable to have any rights in the College aforesaid; and if he shall take a wife after his election, he shall forever lose all rights he may have obtained by such election.

These statutes we have published for the government of our College, and we enjoin that they be diligently and without violation observed by all members thereof; but so that we reserve to ourselves, so long as we shall remain in this life, authority to add to, to take away from, to change, and to interpret them, as often as we shall see just cause arising. In faith and testimony of all which I, the above named Walter Mildmay, have affixed my seal to these presents.

Given on the first day of October, in the year of our Lord one thousand five hundred and eighty-five, and the twenty-seventh year of our most Illustrious Lady Elizabeth, of England, France, and Ireland, Queen etc.

Wa: Mildmay.

NOTES TO CHAPTER 42

The celibacy of Fellows was of course normal in all the Colleges until the latter half of the nineteenth century, and before the Reformation would not have needed stating in respect of Fellows in holy orders. There is no mention of it in the Christ's Statutes, which probably accounts for the present statute standing where it does as apparently an afterthought of the drafters. It may be noted that the prohibition did not apply to the Master.

The statutes contained above in this book were confirmed by the Honourable Sir Walter Mildmay and signed by the same and sealed with his seal; and then delivered to Laurence Chaderton, Master of Emmanuel College in the University of Cambridge, as the statutes of the said College, in the presence of us:

Ant. Mildmay	Hum. Mildmay
Jo. Hammond	Tho. Byng
W. Lewyn	Timothe Bright
	Edmund Downynge

NOTE ON THE DATE AND SEALING OF THE STATUTES

The College site had been conveyed to Mildmay on 23 November 1583; the royal charter authorising the foundation is dated 11 January 1583/4, and Mildmay's deed of foundation 25 May in the same year. When work on the adaptation of the ruinous Dominican buildings for College use began we cannot say; but the first admissions were recorded on 1 November 1584 (E.C.A., CHA.1.4[2]) and eighty names had been inscribed by 1 July 1585. The College seems therefore to have been a going concern by the time the Statutes were signed and sealed by Mildmay on 1 October 1585.

The witnesses to the sealing may be identified as follows:

Anthony Mildmay: The Founder's eldest son and heir. At this time he was M.P. for Wiltshire. In 1596 he served as Ambassador to the French King, Henry IV. He died in 1617.

Humphrey Mildmay: The Founder's second son. He was at this time M.P. for Higham Ferrers. He died in 1613.

John Hammond: Probably the John Hammond who took his LL.D. from Trinity Hall in 1569 and was later Chancellor of the diocese of London. He was a friend of Thomas Byng (see below). He died on 22 December 1589 (see *Trans. Camb. Bib. Soc.*, v, 199).

W. Lewyn: Perhaps William Lewyn, Fellow of Christ's from 1562 to 1571, Judge of the Probate Court of Canterbury 1576 to 1598.

Thomas Byng: He had been a Fellow of Peterhouse at the time that Anthony and Humphrey Mildmay were undergraduates there. He was Master of Clare College from 1571 to 1599, and Regius Professor of Civil Law from 1574 to 1599. He was a friend of the Founder, whom he used to visit at Apethorpe in Northamptonshire. (See *Trans. Camb. Bib. Soc.*, v, 191-202, and esp. 193.)

Timothy Bright: He graduated B.A. from Trinity College in 1567/8, M.D. in 1578/9. In Paris in 1572 he narrowly escaped the St Bartholomew massacre. In 1584 he was in medical practice at Ipswich. Later he took holy orders. He was the inventor of modern shorthand. His brother William became a Fellow of Emmanuel in 1587.

Edmund Downynge: I have failed to identify. He was perhaps a member of the same family as George Downing, Master of Ipswich Grammar School 1589 to 1610, whose son Emmanuel (a Puritan name), born in 1585, migrated to Salem, Massachusetts, and was an ancestor of the Sir George Downing who founded Downing College.

Statute concerning the chamber reserved for kin of the Founder

Since nature has implanted in all men a particular affection for those whom they have themselves begotten, or who are linked to them by the ties of blood, we have thought proper to see to it, as this may be done without detriment to learning, that we may appear in this College also to have had regard to our kin and family. Wherefore we have decided that that single chamber among those recently erected which is the end one of the range, looking eastward, and which lies between the lowest and the highest (nearest the roof), shall be reserved for any of our posterity and kin who shall be admitted to the aforesaid College for the purpose of study. We therefore desire and decree that, if one or more of those who are of our surname and are also by birth descendants of us or of our kinsmen, shall at any time hereafter reside in the said College for the purpose of study, that chamber aforesaid shall be reserved unto them, and that he or they alone shall have free and un-restricted enjoyment of the same, as long as they shall remain in that College, without payment of any compensation or rent for the same. But if there shall be none in the said College of our kin, and of our surname, then if there shall be any one that is a descendant of our daughters, or through them our kin by blood, or if there shall be more than one so qualified, then we desire in like manner that the chamber aforesaid be held and occupied by him or them without any payment of rent or hire, so long as they shall remain in the said College for the purpose of study. But at such times as it shall happen that there be none in the aforesaid College so joined to us by blood as we have before said, we give the Master of the said College full power to assign the same chamber at his discretion to any other person residing in the same College for the purpose of study, always having regard to equity as well as to the dignity and deserts of the person. We desire, however, that anyone not of our kin shall not be assigned the said chamber except on this condition, that he shall vacate the same as soon as any one of those who as we have indicated are to be shown preference shall be admitted and received into the said College for the purpose of study, and shall forthwith relinquish the same to him, to be held by him without pay-ment so long as he shall be in the College; and we desire and command that it be assigned and granted to the same in such case, notwithstanding its having been previously granted to another under the present statute.
December 1587.   Wa: Mildmay

NOTE TO THE STATUTE CONCERNING THE CHAMBER
RESERVED FOR KIN OF THE FOUNDER

The date of this additional statute is of interest. As J. B. Peace showed many years ago (*ECM*, VI, 8ff.), 'we may . . . assume that the Hall, the kitchen, and (for chambers) the old buttressed range that faced Preachers' Street [St Andrew's Street] were the buildings that represented Emmanuel to those who came up in November, 1584'. Accounts for 1587 show that work was still in progress on the old Chapel (now the Old Library), but it is likely that it was complete by the time the dedication festival of the College was held in or about December of that year. The celebrations included solemn thanksgiving and a festive dinner, attended by the Founder in person and by the Vice-Chancellor, Dr Thomas Legge, who afterwards wrote him a formal letter of thanks and congratulations (E.C.A., COL.9.1A[1]). The 'Founder's Range' (now known as the Westmorland Building) was, as this statute shows, recently erected; and it is not unreasonable to suppose that Sir Walter was actually accommodated in the room referred to (in the position of the set now called D3). We may imagine him, on the morning after the dedication, looking out on the Paddock and across the ancient Dominican boundary wall to the open Barnwell fields; and then from the other window (now blocked by the Gallery) into the College he had made, seeing that it was good, and thinking of its future. Of that future he might not himself see many years; but the College would go on, and there would be other Mildmays. He was himself of Christ's; his sons, Anthony and Humphrey, twenty years before, had gone to Peterhouse, when his good friend Thomas Byng was a Fellow there. Another generation might come to Emmanuel; and they should occupy this very room.

*Of the tarrying in the College of the Fellows, and of their
proceeding to the degree of Doctor of Divinity*

Seeing that we have founded our College to the intent that it might be
by the grace of God a seminary of learned men, from which there may
be supplied to the Church as great a number as may possibly be produced therefrom to instruct the people in the Christian religion, we
desire that none of the Fellows suppose that we have given him a
permanent home in that College; and we are the more persuaded that
this must be guarded against for that we have heard many wise and
grave men complain, supporting their opinion by many examples both
from their own memory and of the present time, that the over-long
residence of Fellows in other Colleges has done no little hurt both to
the affairs of the commonwealth and to the interests of the church. For
not only are they themselves almost useless, but they also deprive the
commonwealth of that profit which should accrue through the example
of praiseworthy industry. To the end, therefore, that in the production
of learned men, which we desire to be as plentiful as may be, we may
be seen to have aimed at a rich harvest, and with a view also to the
dignity and reputation of our College, we desire and decree that both
the Master and all the Fellows of the said College, present and future,
see to it that they proceed, as soon as by the public statutes of the
University they can and may, to the degree of Doctor of Divinity. And
if any of them, whether the Master or any one of the Fellows, shall not
have obtained the degree of Doctor of Divinity within that space of
time which is by statute appointed for that degree, then from the next
day of admission to degrees on which he might otherwise have received
his Doctorate, he shall for ever forfeit all present and future tenure of
his place in the College. But after taking the aforesaid degree we desire
that the Master hold office permanently; but we desire that no Fellow
shall hold a Fellowship for more than one year from the day of admission on which he has been duly made a Doctor or on which his Doctorate becomes effective by special grace. But we desire that in reckoning
that year no account be taken of any time during which it shall fall to
any one of them to hold the office of Vice-Chancellor or to perform the
duties of the Regius Professorship of Divinity or of that professorship
founded by the Illustrious Lady Margaret Countess of Richmond and
Derby, provided that these duties be performed in their own name and
right. But as soon as they shall have laid down their office or ceased to

hold the post of these professorships which we have specified, then after the expiry of such number of days as were required, not counting the time of their office or professorship, for the completion of a year, they shall permanently cease to be Fellows. But that those who retire in this manner from our College may not think themselves utterly cast off by us, we desire and decree that, whensoever any benefice under the patronage of our College happens to fall vacant after the retirement of any one of them, it shall be permitted to the Master and Fellows of the said College to present the same to the said benefice (if they think fit) just as if he still held the rights of a Fellow: provided that he do not at that time obtain any other ecclesiastical benefice having the cure of souls attached thereto, or that he effectually relinquish any which he may hold, and that he shall not already have accepted any benefice on the presentation of the College. And even so we do not desire any regard to be had for him unless, in the same manner as has been before ordained by us concerning the presentation of Fellows to benefices, he give surety that he will not accept any other benefice with cure, or requiring personal residence, unless after resigning completely that which he shall obtain on the presentation of the College, and that he will reside in the benefice, as required by the common law, so long as he shall hold it. And lest we should be thought to have been concerned only about the Doctorate of Divinity, and to have neglected other academical degrees, we desire and decree that, if any Fellow of our college aforesaid shall not become a Master of Arts or Bachelor of Divinity within that space of time which is laid down therefor by the statutes of the University, then after the next congregation at which these degrees are customarily conferred upon candidates, he shall be entirely removed from the College, to the permanent exclusion of all expectation of re-election to a Fellowship in the said College; and we desire the same condition to apply to the Master and to all Fellows whose removal, for whatsoever reason, is laid down under our other statutes.

Given on the last day of February, in the year of our Lord one thousand five hundred and eighty-seven, and in the thirtieth year of the most Illustrious Lady Elizabeth, of England, France, and Ireland, Queen, etc.

Wa: Mildmay.

NOTE TO THE STATUTE 'DE MORA SOCIORUM'

This further addition, dated two months after the last, on 28 February 1588, rounds off the book of statutes in the key in which it opened. The prime function of the College was to improve the supply of men fitted for the pastoral ministry of the church. Under chapter 38, Emmanuel men, and especially Fellows, were to be preferred in filling livings of which the College had the patronage. But this extra statute went further, in laying on Fellows an actual obligation to leave the College for pastoral work once they attained the degree of Doctor of Divinity. The statute was peculiar to Emmanuel (though copied at Sidney Sussex six years later), but the view that 'over-long residence of Fellows in other Colleges has done no little hurt both to the affairs of the commonwealth and to the interests of the church' was not peculiar to Mildmay. The Bishops themselves had in 1584 expressed themselves strongly against a petition of the universities to Parliament which aimed to allow Fellows of Colleges to continue in residence for purposes of study despite any statutes which required them to take up pastoral work (cf. Mullinger, *University of Cambridge*, II, pp. 306 ff.).

It was not many years before objection was raised to the *De mora* statute. In 1595 Charles Chadwick, senior Fellow, attempted to retain his Fellowship beyond the allotted time, and argued against the Master (Laurence Chaderton) that this added statute was not of equal validity with the rest. The case was referred to the Vice-Chancellor and the Master of Christ's, who decided against him. That Puritans should dislike the statute was perhaps not due to any objection to preaching or pastoral work, but because they felt that they would be at a disadvantage as candidates for benefices (unless in the gift of the College), and even if successful might have to conform to an intolerable degree to the regulations of an increasingly authoritarian hierarchy.

Things came to a head in 1627, when the Fellows formally petitioned the Crown, proposing that the Heads of Houses should be invited to report on the validity of the statute and the desirability of its modification. The Heads duly reported to the Chancellor (the Duke of Buckingham) that though the statute was legally valid, its provisions were no longer so necessary, since the church was now better supplied with qualified ministers, and Fellows obliged to quit the College might be unable to obtain livings, and be left worse off as Doctors than they had been as Bachelors of Divinity. No other College was so severe on its Fellows, for the similar statute at Sidney Sussex had already been modified. However (they continued), as Sir Henry Mildmay, the Founder's grandson and representative, had expressed willingness to meet the Fellows' needs by himself shortly bestowing on the College the patronage of five or six more benefices, and meanwhile indemnifying any unprovided Fellows by the payment to the College of an annuity of forty marks for each, the petitioners were themselves now content to drop their petition. At the same time Chaderton independently opposed suspension of the statute, stating that the Founder had declared 'he would rather not have founded the College than have omitted this statute', and adding that, while other statutes were suggested to Mildmay by his friends, 'this proceeded solely from himself, and he took more time of deliberation to compose and sett down this statute, than any other'.

The outcome was a royal dispensation, dated 5 May 1627, granting a temporary suspension of the statute, to become permanent unless within six years Sir Henry Mildmay should provide the promised six advowsons. This it appears he did not do.

(The principal documents in the question, down to 1627, are quoted *in extenso* in William Bennet's account of the history of the *De mora* statute in E.C.A., COL.9.1A.

pp. 200–9 and 242. There is a copy of the decision of 1595 in COL.14.1, and a further copy of the royal dispensation in COL.18.28. no. 3.)

In 1640, when the Puritans were in the ascendant, the kindred of the Founder successfully petitioned Parliament to restore the statute, despite the objections of some of the Fellows, who had been elected after its suspension, were now long settled in College, and had no hopes of outside patronage. They claimed that the one year's grace after taking the D.D. was too short a time for them to find a benefice in competition with younger men, and asked that at least the period should be extended. The objectors were unsuccessful, and the statute seems to have remained in force until finally declared of no effect after the Restoration of the Monarchy in 1660.

(A copy of the 1640 petition of the Founder's kin, and what seem to be two separate drafts of the Fellows' objections, are to be found in E.C.A., COL.18.28. nos. 4,1 and 2.)

It is noticeable that Laurence Chaderton, the first Master, who had taken his B.D. degree in 1578, did not conform to this statute by proceeding as soon as possible to the Doctorate. But Dillingham in his life of Chaderton (not published until 1700, but known to have been compiled from materials collected by Archbishop Sancroft from Richard Holdsworth and other members of the College who had known Chaderton well) assures us that the Founder had made a special exception out of regard for his modesty (*quo summae Chadertoni sui modestiae indulgeret*). Chaderton was eventually, in 1613, at the age of about seventy-five, persuaded by royal request to accept a Doctorate on the occasion of the visit of Prince Charles and the Elector Palatine to the University.

The College orders of 1588

Introduction

With the *De mora* statute the Founder could regard his work as complete. There were no further additions or alterations to the statutes in his time. But matters of detail could of course be regulated by order of the Master and Fellows, and at the beginning of the first College order-book (E.C.A., COL.14.1) we find several pages of such regulations dated 10 December 1588. These are of much interest, both for the picture they give of daily life in the College, and for the detailed arrangements agreed upon for 'mutuall conference or communication of gifts among students in Divinity'.

All these orders, printed below, were passed after experience of the first few years' running of the College. To the three Fellows initially appointed in 1584 (Charles Chadwick from Christ's, William Jones and Laurence Pickering from Clare) four more had been added in 1585 (John Cock and Nathaniel Gilby from Christ's, William Branthwaite and John Richardson from Clare), another two (William Bright from Christ's and John Gray from Queens') in 1587, and a further three (John Duke, Richard Rolfe, and Robert Houghton) in 1588, thus bringing the total up to twelve as envisaged in chapter 39 (cf. notes on chapter 11 above). The last three, Duke, Rolfe, and Houghton, had been among the original Scholars at Emmanuel itself: the College had now duly proved itself viable as a self-perpetuating establishment. It was thus an appropriate time to review any regulations or practices that had developed. Whether their codification was carried out at the Founder's behest, we do not know; but it is possible. His last visit to the College of which we have evidence was in July 1588 (the month that saw the defeat of the Spanish Armada). He died on 31 May 1589, between four and five in the afternoon (see *Trans. Camb. Bib. Soc.*, v, 193).

Orders appointed by common consent according to our Statutes for the better government of our Colledge, which because we are persuaded that they are aggreable to Gods word necessarie for the discharge of our duties imposed upon us by our Honourable Founder and his statutes, and not repugnant to any law civill or ecclesiasticall in the lande: we purpose and promise to keep so long as we shalbe thus persuaded. For if we were not thus persuaded, we wolde not make or keep them: nether will we keep them longer then we may be warranted by all these.

Anno. 1588. Decemb. 10.

Office of 4 Ministers: Memorandum that wheras the Statute requireth the Maister and fower Fellows to be Ministers, all the Society desires that the Maister and Mr Jones would principally endevour by exhortation to applie the doctrine of Religion to the present state of the Colledge and to administer the Sacraments. And that Mr Chadwick Mr Pickering and Mr Cock would especially endevour to teache sound doctrine and confute errour, at other times then onely when they are bound by Statute of the University and of the Colledge so to doe.

Meeting day appointed. Item it is aggreed that there shalbe a meeting of the society together the first Tuesday in every moneth at one of the clocke in the afternoon to consider of such matters as are amisse in the Colledge ether belonging to the dean's office or the Lecturer's or any misorder in the house that they may be amended according to our statutes, and to receive information of all in the Colledge.

Inspection Item that Mr Richardson is desired to look to all that goe up and down his stayre to their lodging and to the kitchin. Mr Gylby to those within Mr Chadwick his door and Mr Pickering's. Mr Branthwayt to all those in the rest of the range to the other end Mr Bright to all those that are lodged from his own chamber to Mr Jones. Mr Gray to those that enter in at his own and Mr Jones his dore. Mr Duke to all over and under himself and those under and above the Master's lodgings.

Inspection.
Item that Mr Richardson and Mr Gylby are desired especially to look to disorders and all undecency committed in the chappell and in the hall at all times. Mr Branthwait and Mr Bright to disorders and ill behaviour in the courts and backsides. Mr Gray and Mr Duke to enquire of such as goe often out of the Colledge or tary long forth or frequent houses in the Town.

Almes at Communion.
Moreover that Mr Rolfe and Mr Houghton are desired to gather at every Communion according to the statute of the land the Almes of the Communicants and to signifie on the sixt Tuesday after the beginning of every quarter to all the society whome they think to be prest or sick that they may be releived therewith.

Communion when?
Item it is agreed of all to have the Communion the third Sunday in every terme after the beginning of the same.

Questionists sitt.
Item that the Questionists shold sitt the 13 and 14 of Januarie to be opposed from one a clock till three in the afternoon in the Parlour.

Bookes for Lectures
Item that the books thought necessarie to have redd through [be] Ramus Logick Aristotles Organon Ethicks Politiques and Physiques: and if they can or will they may read Phrigius his naturall Philosophie.

Coming into the hall.
Item that all the fellows shall immediately after the ringing of the bell to dinner and supper come to sit down at the table that the fellocommoners may sit down also in their place.

Butler.
Item that the butler shall not take any mony for any sizing whatsoever nor deliver mony for any allowance.

Kitchin.
Item that no schollar at any time for any cause the Stuards onely excepted shall come into the Kitchin nether any stranger man woman boye or gyrle.

Commons.
Item that upon warning given all in the house without exception of any shall pay their mony for commons to

the Stuard before hand as the statute appointeth in that point, and so begin at Michaelmas next without fayll. aggreed Aug. 29. 1589 [*sic*]

These decrees above written according to statute are appointed to be observed by common consent of the Mr and all the fellows.

NOTES

Office of 4 Ministers: cf. chapters 9 and 21.

Communion: Chapter 20 requires celebration of Holy Communion at least once a term.

Questionists: i.e., undergraduates due to come up for University examination (by maintaining a question or thesis, in formal disputation) in the Lent Term. This preliminary session on 13 and 14 January was a College qualifying examination.

Bookes for lectures: Mediaeval education, in placing at the head of the curriculum the formal study of logic, or more specifically of Aristotle's works on logic, had recognised the importance of logical reasoning as a necessary process in the acquisition of any true knowledge. But there is a deal of difference between logical thought and the academic discussion and analysis of the process. Petrus Ramus (Pierre de la Ramée), 1515–72, attacked Aristotelian logic as an abstract and unnecessarily artificial formulation of the natural rules of reasoning. His new approach, first adumbrated in his M.A. thesis at Paris in 1536, rapidly gained ground, and after his conversion to Calvinism became especially successful in the Protestant universities of Europe. It had a very strong (though not unopposed) following in sixteenth-century Cambridge, partly on account of Chaderton's own lectures, according to Dillingham's life (trans. E. S. Shuckburgh, *Laurence Chaderton, D.D. . . .*, p. 5); and a duodecimo edition of Ramus's *Dialecticae libri duo* was one of the first books printed by Thomas Thomas on the revival of the Cambridge University Press under the protection of Lord Burghley in the year of the foundation of Emmanuel. It is interesting that although Ramus is here given pride of place the Lecturer is still expected to expound also the logical works of Aristotle (collectively, the *Organon*).

Phrigius his naturall Philosophie is doubtless the *Quaestiones physicae* – a compendium of all the natural sciences – of Johann Thomas Freig (Freigius). Freig was a prolific writer and editor of books for university students on many subjects. The phrase 'if they can or will' has a certain poignancy in face of the 1579 Basel edition of the *Quaestiones*, which runs to 1,295 pages and bears the epigraph *in magnis et voluisse sat est* – 'in great matters the will is enough'.

Decrees agreed upon by the Master and Fellows
for the better government of the Colledge

Hall. 1.   Memorandum that it is agreed by common consent that every scholler absent from praier before or after meate or carying away his part out of the hall without leave to any place shall pay the price of it. and that the understuard shold note it and give accompts thereof every Saturday at the casting of commons.

Visiting. 2.   Item it is appointed that the ordinary visiting of chambers shold be done by two, viz. one senior and one iunior fellow at one time both together, according to the forme prescribed in statute.

Diner time. 3.   Item it is aggreed alwaies to dine at eleven of the clock.

Recreation. 4.   Item it is appointed and aggreed upon by common consent that the times of recreation are, one houre after dinner, and after supper, viz. till one, and seven: also one houre before supper (unless some publique exercise of learning or religion doe require their presence) And that all other times shold be spent in their calling: or els to be admonished and corrected according to statute.

Vessells. 5.   Item that no fellow scholler pensioner syser or subsizer or any other within the colledge doe take and cary out of the Kitchin into his chamber study or any other place in the Colledge or keep them there being brought by others any manner of vessell save only into the hall at dinner and supper time. Provided for the better performance hereof and by common consent aggreed that the fellows shall have vessell distributed amongst them to the value of six pounds which they shall make good unto the colledge at their departure if any be lost or molten.

Butler. 6.   Item that the butler come in halfe an hower before 8 in the morning and shut his dore at 8. Again to come in a little before three and to shut up at the stroke of three. Lastly at 7 after supper and to shut up at 8. At which times the butler onely shall toull the bell, according to th' order: as also he shall ring at dinner and supper.

Against 7.
Slovenliness.
     Yf any scholler doe take an other making water in any place of the Colledge or near the gates save onely there where it is or shalbe appointed for that end, he shall have ijd allowed upon his heade. The same mulct also he shall have if he find any emptying chamber potts, or abusing any place about the Colledge with any manner of uncleannes.

Theis orders before written in this leafe are ordayned and appointed, to bee continually observed by common consent of the Master and Fellowes, as apeareth by the subscription of their handes. Anno Dni. 1588. Decemb. 10.

> Laurence Chaderton
> Char. Chadwick
> William Jones
> Laur. Pickering
> John Cock
> John Richardson
> Nathaniel Gylbie
> William Branthwayte
> William Bright
> John Graye
> Jhon Duke
> Richard Rolfe
> Robert Houghton

NOTES

This further group of regulations (numbered 1 to 7) about domestic details are in the order-book placed after the orders for 'mutuall conference' printed and discussed below. It is possible that the pages have been rearranged in the binding; in any case they belong in subject-matter more closely with those already discussed, and they have therefore been transposed for the purposes of the present edition.

Recreation: This order, taken with the regulation for the Butler's opening times, and some other information, gives the following approximate time-table for a typical weekday:

Morning prayers	
?6.30–7.30	Lectures in Hall (chapter 29)
7.30–8.00	Buttery open for bevers (see chapter 35, note)
[8.00–11.00	Study]
11.00	Dinner

12.00–1.00	Recreation
[1.00–2.50	Study]
2.50–3.00	Buttery open for bevers
[3.00–5.00	Study]
?5.00–6.00	Recreation (unless prevented by academic exercises, e.g., 4–6 on Fridays, disputation in Theology; see chapter 14).
?6.00	Supper
7.00–8.00	Recreation; buttery open.
8.00 (9.00 in summer)	College gates locked (chapter 6)
Tutor's prayers.	

Vessells: The earliest inventories of the College furniture, utensils, etc., dated 1589 (in E.C.A., BUR.8.1, printed in *ECM*, XLII, 35–41) show that the equipment of the house was modest, even austere; and there was doubtless need to keep careful note of it all. At that date we have unfortunately no list showing what was on charge to individual Fellows. Fifty years later, it was normal for each to hold for his own use a tankard (for fetching drink from the buttery), a stoop (i.e., beaker), a spoon, and sometimes a 'wine-bowl' and a trencher salt. These were of silver, and the 1588 order seems to envisage some similar 'issue' of plate to Fellows. The quite large sum of six pounds (contrast the amount of a Fellow's annual cash-allowance in chapter 23 – thirty shillings) would at the then current price of five shillings per fine ounce be equivalent to twenty-four ounces of silver – enough in fact for a tankard, stoop, and spoon. However, in the 1589 inventory the only silver listed (apart from the Master's silver-gilt covered cup) is three bowls for beer or wine, six bellied pots, two salts, and two dozen spoons.

A mutuall conference in communication of giftes
among Students in Divinity confirmed
by the Canonicall
Scriptures.

1. Cor. 14.29   The Apostle having laboured in this Chapter (1. Cor. 14.29) to draw the Corinthians to a greater estimation, and more diligent use, of the gift of Prophecy; as a thing most profitable, to the edification of the Churche: now hee prescribeth them a very good and profitable course, for the right use of this gift, to the greater benefitt of themselves, and of the Churche. Which course standeth in theis points. 1. That two or three at one meeting should speake. 2. That the rest of the Prophets present shold judge of that which was spoken, whither it were sound and agreable to the word or no: to th' end that if it were sound, they might give the doctrine their allowance, that so it mought bee of more authority: yf not; that the speaker might brotherly bee admonished of it, and the churche take no hurt thereby. 3. Yf any thinge were revealed to him that sat by, the first should hold his peace. 4. That every of the Prophets should in his course bee admitted to speake, as order and the Churches good would permitt. Lastly, that such as had spoken, should willingly submitt them selves, and doctrine, to the judgement and censure of the whole company of Prophets; and bee content to bee advised, or reformed (yf need were) by their discreet and brotherly censure. This course prescribed by the Apostle, beeing generally set down, and not appropriated to the Churche, or tyme, no more then the calling of Prophets; and having a good and necessary use, wheresoever there is (as was in Corinth) a number of Prophets, or sonnes of the Prophets together: wee thinke it laieth hold on us; yf not in every circumstaunce, yet in the substaunce of the action.

And for as muche, as wee being enjoyned by statute, have with one consent, admitted this order thus farre, as to speake every one, and that in course (though not so many at a time, as th' Apostle requireth by reason of other business which is not to bee neglected: nor by immediat use of revelation because that gift is ceased) wee think it of absolute necessity that there bee also among us. 1. A judging on their parts that do heare which is the second point before mentioned. And this judging to bee not a deeming in every mans mynd what is to be thought of matters propounded by the speaker and going no further, but a free judgment delivered by speache, approving that which wee take to bee sound, and with good reason disalowing that which is otherwise, to the end that hee which hath spoken may bee the better confirmed by our consents in the truth hee hath delivered: or yf need require by our advice reformed in his judgment in suche points as hee hath swerved from the same. 2. That the Speaker do willingly submitt him selfe and his judgment to the judgment and censure of the rest and bee content upon good ground and reason rendered either to reforme his opinion, or at least to cease from further publishing of it untill it please God to reveale more clearly the trueth in such matters.

For having admitted one part of the precept, wee can not refuse th' other, unlesse wee will take liberty to allow and refuse where wee list, and indeed to separate those things which the Lord would have go jointly together.

1. Thess. 5.21   Againe th' Apostle 1. Thess. 5.21 commaunding all Christians to try the Doctrine delivered unto them by Prophets, doth muche more bynde the Prophets them selves who not only bee present at such prophecies but also do live together to examine and try suche doctrine as is delivered.

1. Joh. 4.1   The same duty doth St John 1. ep. cap. 4 lay on all Christians and in them on the Prophets to try the spirits whither they bee of God or no. And after every suche triall soundly made, as thei are bound for the benefit of the Churche to give their consents and lyking to all that which is agreable to holsome doctrine so are

they bound by the Apostles' precepts in other places to admonish the Speaker of such scapes or errors wherein he failed in preaching the Word, for St Paul chargeth all the Christians Col. 3.16 to teache and admonish one another: and in the 1. Thess. 5.11 to exhort and edify one another. Yf all Christians must performe their duties unto all, then doubtlesse Prophets must do it unto their fellow-Prophets: and that as in all the parts of their lives so especially in their preachings yf they mark any thing come from them which is not agreable to sound doctrine: that beeing admonished of their severall faults and taught how to amend them they may grow daily unto a greater ripenes and perfection in that honorable calling wherein they serve the Lord.

1. Cor. 12.7 Moreover St Paul 1. Cor. 12.7 having shewed that there bee divers gifts of the Spirit in the Churche of God: doth set down, why the Spirit doth so plenteously bestow his graces, which is πρὸς τὸ συμφέρον for the good and benefit of the whole body, and every member thereof. And vs. 25 after hee had shewed, how as in the body, so in the Churche, those who had the best guiftes shold not contemne others which had the meanest; he requireth this of all the members, that they all have a mutuall care for the good of the whole Churche, and of every member therein; according as in the body every member is carefull to procure the good and benefit of the rest of the members. Wherein this duty is layd on every one of us, that wee do not every one look to him selfe, and neglect others; but all bestow our care and studie, in furthering the good of another, even in that kynd, wherein his goodnes doth consist.

And having receaved any giftes of the Spirit, profitable for the whole Churche, or any member thereof, whither it bee the gift of judgment, to judge of sound doctrine; or of discretion, to discerne of the maner of delivery; or of interpretation, to fynd out the true sense and meaning of the Scripture; we are by the Apostles rule, to use theis giftes, to the good of others.

And from this generall duty wee derive this speciall that every one of us in this assemblie are bound by the Apostles precept to use our gifts then when wee see necessary use of them: whiche is then especially when the word hath been expounded by any of our fellow-prophets. That yf any doctrine or exhortacon bee propounded that is not sound in it selfe or not surely grounded on the place whence hee draweth it wee do by judgement disalow it; yf the maner of delivery bee defective, wee by discretion seeke to reforme; yf the interpretation bee untrue or unfitt for the place, wee do by the gift God hath given us set down a better.

And for the Speaker wee thinke that hee is bound not only to heare th' advice and judgment of others willingly but even to desire it of his own accord for his surer direction and better confirmation in a sound maner of teaching by that whiche th' Apostle com-

1. Cor. 3.10   maundeth 1. Cor. 3.10. Let every man looke what hee buildeth on the foundation. For in theis wordes th' Apostle layeth great awe upon such as were builders to bee very carefull how they builded. And the reason hee addeth from the daunger of an yll maner of building doth more enforce this duty upon them. For yf hee that buildeth wood straw or stubble upon the foundation is sure to suffer loss of all his worke, so as it shalbe none otherwise with him then yf hee had not builded at all, then doubtlesse men must use all care and all good meanes both in them selves and out of them selves to come to such a sound maner of building that their worke they have builded abyding, they may receave the reward of wise builders.

Act. 18.24   A practise of both theis we have Act: 18.24 in that Apollos was content to bee further enstructed and more fully taught in the way of the Lord by Priscilla and Aquila two persons of inferior gifts and calling, that wee might be the better enhabled to teache more fully. And they seeing his defect which made his Ministery of lesse force thought it their duty to enforme him further.

Seeing then wee have sufficient ground out of the Word for that which wee have taken in hand: which may both warrant our own consciences and afford a just defence of our doings unto all [who] shall ask us a reason of the same: our next care must bee to practise this order in suche a maner and sort as may bee fittest for our mutuall edifying one of another. Whiche shalbee done, yf every one laying aside all pride and contempt, all vaine glory and desire to seeme somwhat, all hard and uncharitable speaches and generally all sinister affections do with humility meekness and love behave him selfe in our assembly and meetings as th' Apostle willeth the Christians to walk Eph. 4.2. 2 Tim. 3.25. Tit. 3.2. Gal. 5.13 and 6.1. Eph. 4.15.

Moreover, for the more orderly discharging of all theis duties, and for the better avoyding of all suche occasions as may breed any suspitions, or renting of myndes and wills asunder: wee have all with one consent agreed upon all theis articles following.

1. That all of us do meet together at seven of the clock the same day that any exercise hath been.
2. That a praier be made both at the beginning and the end by the Master him selfe: or in his absence by the senior of them which bee present.
3. That in propounding any point to bee considered of, the senior beginne and so the rest in order.
4. That first they consider of the doctrine and then of the maner of teaching.
5. That none do conceale his mislyke but with the reason thereof to submitt it to the judgment of the rest.
6. That the Master or in his absence the senior of them that are present do signify the judgment of the company in their hearing, unto him that hath spoken, before wee proceed to any other busines.
7. That none reveale unto the party censured, who it was that found fault with him; because the judgement is the judgement of all and not of any one alone.

8. That no man which is not of the company bee made
party to that whiche is done amongst us.

                            Anno Dni 1588. Decemb. 10
This order of Conference before written, with the
maner of using the same, is ordayned and apointed to
bee continually observed by common consent of the
Master and the fellowes, as apeareth by their handes.
Anno Dni. 1588. Decemb. 10.

> Laurence Chaderton
> Charles Chadwick
> William Jones
> Laur. Pickeringe
> John Cock
> John Richardson
> Nathaniel Gylbie
> William Branthwayte
> William Bright
> John Graye
> Jhon Duke
> Richard Rolfe
> Robert Houghton.

NOTE TO THE ORDER 'A MUTUALL CONFERENCE'

These pages should be understood as amplification of chapter 21. There a weekly
disputation in Theology had been prescribed; but the Master and Fellows were
authorised to lay down 'such more fruitful manner of exercises as they shall decide
to be most convenient for the promotion of . . . Theology and for the training of
ministers of the word'. What is now described corresponds to the 'exercises of
prophesying' which had grown up among Puritans in Elizabethan England on the
pattern devised in the 1520s by Zwingli for his Protestant theological college at
Zürich. The essential was a regular and concentrated study of the Bible. Interpretation of the text was not to be bound by tradition, but the element of mutual criticism
was to check idiosyncratic or unsound doctrine and to promote uniformity. In
Elizabethan England, meetings of the parochial clergy for such 'prophesyings',
though not organised by authority of the Bishops, nevertheless by the 1570s were
receiving widespread episcopal approval. The Queen, however, saw them as
inimical to uniformity, and in 1576 issued a peremptory order that they should
cease. Archbishop Grindal's fall was immediately provoked by his refusal to be her
instrument for their suppression. (See Patrick Collinson, *The Elizabethan Puritan
Movement*, pp. 167, 168–90.)

Laurence Chaderton had already developed a similar scheme for the training of
students of Divinity during his time at Christ's College, making it 'a Puritan seminary

in all but name' (Collinson, pp. 125ff.). A MS preserved in Dr Williams's Library (printed in part by A. Peel in *The Seconde Parte of a Register* . . . (Cambridge, 1915), pp. 133f.) includes a document endorsed 'orders for a Conference used by Mr Chaderton at Cambridge', apparently datable to the 1570s. Its full title is 'An order to be used for the trayning upp and exercising of Students in Divinitye, whereby they maybe made fitt and meete to dyscharge the dewtyes belonging to that profession'. The instructions therein for 'mutuall conference' more explicitly define how the whole Bible is to be subjected to detailed study over a two-year course, making use of the 'gifts' of knowledge of Greek and Hebrew, Rhetoric, and Logic; comparison of other passages of Scripture; study of earlier commentaries; and knowledge of ancient history. After exhaustive examination of the text, two students are to deliver in speech their resultant understanding of the meaning; the rest to hear and judge. Then, if there is dissent, particular issues should be subjected to formal disputation 'as usual in the Universities'.

The similarity to the present orders is plain; and there can be no doubt that Chaderton, as Master, was primarily responsible for these arrangements at Emmanuel. The lengthy justification from Scripture shows a deeply serious sense of these study sessions as vital to the purpose of the foundation, and at the same time indicates that the College were prepared if necessary to defend themselves against any suggestion from civil or ecclesiastical authority that what they were doing was unorthodox or illegal.

Statuta D. Gualtheri Mildmaii Militis Cancellarii Scaccarii et Regineae Maiestati a consiliis: quae pro administratione Collegii Emmanuelis ab eo fundati sancivit

Praefatio

Vetus in Ecclesia Dei institutum est, et ab antiquissimis ductum temporibus, ut scholae atque collegia instituantur Juventuti in omni pietate et bonis literis, praecipue vero in sacris et theologicis educandae, quae sic informata alios postea veram et puram religionem doceat, haereses, et errores omnes refutet, atque praeclarissimis vitae integerrimae exemplis ad virtutem omnes excitet. Sic enim in sacra historia legimus Naiothis, Gilgali, Betheli, Jerechunti, prophetarum filios a summis et celeberrimis prophetis Samuele, Elia, Elizaeo, ad Dei nomen praedicandum, et populum de vera religione informandum, institutos fuisse. Jerusolimis vero plurimas, et singularum fere nationum proprias synagogas fuisse in Actis Apostolorum memoratur: ad quas undique ex toto fere terrarum orbe, tanquam ad mercaturam quandam religionis literarum atque virtutum confluebant. Inter quos et Saulus ille Tarsensis (qui postea Paulus dictus est) lectissimum Domini instrumentum et gentium doctor, ad reverendi viri Gamalielis pedes assedisse dicitur. Intellexerunt enim viri divino spiritus instinctu afflati, non posse Evangelii lucem diffundi in omnem posteritatem ad Dei gloriam, et hominum salutem, nisi in ipsius Ecclesia tanquam in horto paradisi efficerentur et adornarentur quaedam Theologiae, atque optimarum artium, quasi nobilissimarum plantarum φυτευτήρια, ex quibus qui ad maturitatem excreverint transferrentur in omnes partes Ecclesiae, quo illa horum sudore rigata et Dei nostri incremento aucta, tandem ad florentissimum beatissimumque statum perveniret. Quemadmodum enim ad ignem caelitus demissum (quo solo ad sacrificia super altare

comburenda uti licebat) custodes Levitae adhibebantur, qui eum
assidue foverent et conservarent, ita et vera Dei cognitio (quasi ignis e
caelo delapsus) assiduis vigiliis et operibus asservanda et fovenda est,
ne alienum ignem, puta Papismum, caeterasque haereses ex terra et
hominum commentis ortas ad incendendum coram Domino odores
afferamus. Atque, ut reliqua terrae irrigandae flumina ex Edeni horti
fontibus manabant, ita scholae quasi fontes quidam aperiendi sunt, qui
e Paradiso Dei orti omnes terrae nostrae, adeoque totius orbis regiones
purissimae doctrinae fidei, et sanctissimae disciplinae morum tanquam
aureo flumine rigare possint. Itaque tam divina et antiqua prophetarum
Dei instituta a maioribus nostris multi heroica virtute viri imitati,
collegia et σοφῶν ψυχῶν φροντιστήρια Deo et Ecclesiae posuerunt,
quorum magnificentiam et regios sumptus aequare concedens aliis, qui
propius ad tantae munificentiae honorem possint accedere, mihi satis
esse puto eorum virtutes imitari, a quibus cum alia quamplurima, tum
huius etiam laudis exempla accepimus, et pro mea facultate religionis ac
vitae puritatem ad posteros nostros propagare. Cum vero nulla tam
parva societas sit, quae vel certo ordine regi vel diu consistere possit,
nisi legitima quaedam eius moderandae et continendae ratio atque
disciplina statuatur: ideo omnibus totius collegii nostri et singulorum
certis officiis describendis edicta et statuta quaedam in sua capita
distincta constituemus quibus omnes nostros subjici et parere volumus.

CAP. I
De Magistri Authoritate

Et quoniam a capite iustum est exordiri a quo regi et administrari
caetera membra decet, primum de Magistro statuamus quem tanquam
caput sociis et scholaribus omnibus esse volumus. Laurentio itaque
Chadertono, in sacra Theologia Baccalaureo, qui iam mea authoritate
Magister antedicti collegii est institutus, atque etiam caeteris omnibus
illius successoribus (cuique pro tempore suo) authoritatem tribuimus
in socios et scholares omnes eiusdem collegii, eosdem gubernandi,
regendi, puniendi, admonendi, et rem domesticam totius collegii
administrandi, iuxta ordinationes et statuta praesentia a me edita, quae
sequuntur inferius. Non licebit tamen eidem Laurentio, nec alicui
successorum eius, absque expresso consensu maioris partis sociorum,
tum in Universitate praesentium, querelam, placitum, aut aliam actionem
quamcunque sub nomine collegii attemptare, per se neque per alium

quemlibet, neque terras, tenementa, decimas, oblationes, aut caeteras possessiones eiusdem collegii, sive temporales, sive spirituales, iam collatas aut in posterum conferendas, alienare sive ad firmam demittere: neque officium, feodum, aut pensionem aliquam de bonis, terris, aut tenementis collegii praedicti cuiquam concedere: neque ecclesiarum earum (quae ad patronatum antedicti collegii pertinent) praesentationes conferre; neque negotium aliquod, ex quo dedecus aut incommodum collegio dicto oriri possit, aggredi, nec confirmare, aut terminare: nisi ex maioris partis Magistri ipsius et sociorum eiusdem collegii assensu. Quod vero maior pars ex Magistro et sociis praedictis egerit, sive in his praedictis sive in aliis quibuslibet (quod ordinationibus et statutis nostris non repugnat) ratum et gratum haberi volumus et statuimus. Emolumenta quae proveniunt ex concessionibus singulis in publicum collegii usum conferri volumus, et nullo modo in privatos usus cedere; ita tamen ut neminem in ballivum, receptorem, aut firmarium admittant, qui non fidei iussores idoneos dederit Magistro et sociis praedictis pro collegii in ea parte indemnitate. Damus etiam Magistro praedicto potestatem tempora studiorum ac etiam animi remittendi scholarium et Pensionariorum omnium pro sua prudentia moderandi.

CAP. 2
De residentia Magistri

Quando etiam capiti convenit, ut caeteris uniatur membris, volumus et statuimus, quod nec praedictus Magister qui nunc est, nec futurorum aliquis in ullis aliis praeterquam ipsius collegii negotiis absit ab eodem ultra spatium unius mensis in singulis anni quartis, sub poena amissionis magistratus sui ipso facto. Quo tempore nihil ei pro commeatu aut caeteris expensis allocabitur ex sumptibus dicti collegii. Licebit ei tamen in urgentibus causis et negotiis necessariis eiusdem collegii diutius abesse, prout necessitas postulabit, sed omnino ipsius conscientiam oneramus in Domino, ut suam absentiam non coloret, neve excuset ullo modo praetextu negotiorum ipsius collegii, nisi eiusmodi fuerint, quae diutinam ipsius absentiam exposcant revera, nisi etiam aegrotatione aliqua ingenti, aut violenta detentione forte impeditus fuerit, quam legitime probaverit coram Procancellario universitatis praedictae, seu vices eius gerenti, ac duobus in sacra Theologia Doctoribus residentibus, et altero eorum assentiente eidem Procancellario in causae ipsius approbatione, si de absentia sua quaestionem ei ab aliquo sociorum moveri contigerit. In caeteris necessitatibus quae abditae sunt, et quas Magister aperire noluerit, satis esse volumus, si pernecessariam et valde urgentem causam se habuisse iuraverit in praesentia Procancellarii seu vices eius gerentis et maioris partis sociorum, ut tunc e quarta anni succedente dies tot assumere possit ultra mensem praedictum, quot ei necessarii videbuntur, sic tamen, ut in hac necessitate universa ipsius absentia spatium duorum mensium intra unam unius anni medietatem non exuperet.

CAP. 3
De modo coercendi

Sed ne forte nimia capitis severitas in membrorum vergat perniciem, hac moderatione Magistrum uti volumus et statuimus, ut in omnibus eiusmodi correctionibus per eum exercendis Decanum et socium seniorem (quorum officia inferius describemus) ad se vocabit, utpote visuros et audituros quicquid in eis rebus fecerit, ut (quoties opus fuerit) tanquam testes idonei citari possint totius rei gestae inter Magistrum et personam puniendam. Nam volumus ut si Magistrum praedictum persona illa senserit in se nimis severum, tunc eidem licebit ad Procancellarium universitatis seu eius vices gerentem appellare. Et si Procancellarius aut eius vices gerens, citata utraque parte, et re audita ex relatione Decani et senioris socii, assistentibus duobus in sacra Theologia Doctoribus maxime senioribus, sive in Doctorum absentia in Theologia Baccalaureis maxime senioribus, atque ex iudicio alterius eorum repererit personam illam iustam appellandi causam habere, sine mora iubeat Magistrum illi iniustae vexationi supersedere. Sin autem contra personam illam inique appellasse repererit, ex iudicio etiam Doctorum aut Baccalaureorum sibi assistentium, tunc sententia Magistri in personam prius lata robur suum et validam teneat firmitatem. Quod si per appellantem steterit, quo minus causa appellationis sive querelae praedictae intra duas hebdomadas terminetur, tunc appellationem praedictam pro deserta et irrita haberi volumus, nec ulterius eandem prosequendi habeat facultatem. In criminalibus vero, si quis sociorum aut Scholarium domestico iudicio non contentus, causam per modum appellationis deferat ad Procancellarium, et audita causa in huiusmodi negotio succubuerit, is, utpote latae culpae reus et tranquillitatis perturbator, e collegio nostro eiiciatur.

CAP. 4
De praeferendis probis et de camerarum assignatione

Caeterum, ut improbi poenis debent coerceri a vitiis, ita probi praemiis provocandi sunt ad virtutes. Volumus igitur et statuimus, ut Magister illos, quos viderit religioni, doctrinae et probitati diligentius insudare, humanius tractet et mollius, eosdemque semper praeferat, quoad potest, et seniores secundum admissionem maxime (caeteris paribus) in cunctis rebus tam ad collegium quam ad universitatem pertinentibus, quae poterunt eis vel emolumento vel ornamento esse: ut in muneribus sive domesticis sive publicis gerendis, in ecclesiarum et beneficiorum collationibus, in camerarum assignationibus, in quibus quaternos cubare volumus e scholaribus, neminemque alium praeter socios unam cameram in suum proprium usum habere. Magistro ipsi pro tempore existenti cameras assignamus, quas ad usum Magistri aedificari procuravimus. Omnium vero camerarum mercedem, quae a pensionariis solis exigetur, in usum collegii convertendam statuimus. Mercedis summam constituet Magister assistentibus ei duobus maxime senioribus sociis.

CAP. 5
De computo reddendo

Consentaneum est etiam, ut socii omnes collegii ipsius statum non ignorent. Statuimus igitur, quod Magister singulis annis ad duo tempora, semel intra mensem a festo Paschae, atque iterum etiam intra mensem alium a festo Divi Michaelis Archangeli, sociis omnibus antea per triduum admonitis, et tunc praesentibus, aut saltem maiori parti eorundem computum reddat veracem et fidelem de cunctis ad officium et administrationem spectantibus, quid expenderit, quid receperit, et quid supersit recipiendum, quid collegium debeat, et quid vicissim debeatur eidem. Ballivos et firmarios eodem tempore suos computos facere cogat: thesaurum universum, iocalia omnia ac caetera munimenta ostendat sociis illis omnibus, rursumque reponat, eis praesentibus, intra Thesaurarium in scriniis ad hoc deputatis. Fieri quoque volumus per eundem singulis quibusque temporibus dictorum computorum indenturas duas statum eiusdem collegii manifeste continentes, quarum alteram in communi cista reponi iubemus cum pecunia ipsa, quae post computum superesse contigerit, alteram in Magistri ipsius custodia retineri. Et si forte Magister computum statutis temporibus non reddiderit, aut sociis in reddendo computo non satisfecerit, tum rem ad Procancellarium universitatis seu vices eius gerentem, referri volumus: qui duobus ad se accitis in sacra Theologia Doctoribus, aut ob eorum absentiam, Baccalaureis in eadem senioribus, partem aberrantem iuxta suam discretionem reformet. Liberum tamen Magistro esse volumus, ut si crescentibus collegii praedicti redditibus, velit se onere colligendorum eorum reddituum computosque eo nomine reddendi eximere, possit alicui ex sociis praedicti collegii cum consensu maioris partis sociorum hoc munus delegare, quem sic designatum redditus praedictos recipere, et computum de receptis et expensis in ea parte temporibus, quae dicto Magistro ad statum collegii praedicti patefaciendum caeteraque praemissa facienda sunt assignata, reddere volumus.

CAP. 6
De tuta rerum custodia

Et quo tutius ac securius res ipsius collegii custodiri queant, volumus et statuimus, ut in thesaurario cista quaedam ampla sit, quae communis cista appellabitur, in qua universa ipsius collegii pecunia reponetur una cum cistula quadam exigua ad sigilli communis custodiam deputata, cuius cistulae clavem Magister ipse geret. Sintque aliae cistae in eodem thesaurario pro conservandis iocalibus caeterisque rebus quae ad necessarios usus spectabunt; ea vero quae in quotidiano usu sunt Magister ipse curet loco aliquo tuto custodiri. Sint etiam in eodem thesaurario scrinia quaedam, in quibus chartas, literas patentes, confirmationes, evidentias, indenturas, obligationes, et caetera munimenta ad ipsum collegium spectantia, inventorium quoque rerum omnium, atque haec originalia statuta recondi volumus. Erunt praeterea cuiusque cistae tres serulae cum tribus clavibus diversarum fabricarum, quarum primam Magister ipse servabit sive eius locum tenens, secundam senior socius, qui pro tempore fuerit, tertiam custos cistae communis, de quorum officiis dicemus postea: volumus igitur, et statuimus, quod istarum rerum (quas supra enumeravimus) nihil cuiquam mutuetur. Et si quando ad usum collegii necessarium efferendae sint, prius inde schedula conficiatur manu ipsius recipientis, quae intra cistam communem remanere debet donec eaedem ipsae res rursum integre restituantur: quod proximo die fieri volumus post finitum earum necessarium usum: singulis etiam noctibus ianuas omnes et ostia collegii ab hora octava in hyeme et ab hora nona in aestate, Magister seu eius locum tenens obserari curabit, et claves eorum singulas ad se deferri.

CAP. 7
De Magistri stipendio

Et ne forte tot labores incassum a Magistro ipso absque emolumento subeantur, volumus et statuimus, quod Magister quisque pro tempore suo suscipiat pro opera administrationis suae, scilicet pro stipendio suo annuo, viginti libras ad duos anni terminos consuetudinarios, aequis portionibus ei singulis annis persolvendas: pro vestitura autem singulis annis tres libras, novem solidos, et quatuor denarios: pro communiis vero hebdomadariis duos solidos singulis hebdomadis et pro famuli sui stipendio singulis annis viginti sex solidos et octo denarios; Magistro etiam assignamus, et in proprium usum illi concedimus hortum unum, columbarium, et herbagium omnium terrarum infra ambitum ipsius collegii, excepto sociorum pomario.

CAP. 8
De Magistri vicario

Cum autem Magistro permiserimus aliquandiu a praedicto collegio abesse, aequum est ut de administratore aliquo in eius absentia provideatur. Volumus igitur et statuimus, ut sive absente magistro, seu magistratu ipsius vacante, sociorum aliquis semper administret: in absentia quidem ille quem Magister assignare voluerit: in vacatione vero socius ipse qui iuxta admissionem senior fuerit: vicariam authoritatem uterque obtineat tempore suo, et tam in sociis congregandis, quam in consiliis tractandis ob utilitatem et honorem ipsius collegii praesideat, et primus sit, eique tanquam Magistro pareatur: hoc excepto, quod neuter eorum electiones ullas faciet aut sociorum aut discipulorum, nec cameras alicui assignabit, neque literas aliquas sigillo communi consignabit, vel consignatas cuiquam tradet, praeter eas duntaxat quae ad Magistri electi praesentationem attinent. Socius item ipse senior tempore vacationis de redditibus collegii recipiendis aut debitis aliis non se intromittet, sed per maiorem partem sociorum quispiam ex universo numero designabitur, cuius erit de rebus eiusmodi collegio respondere, et de rebus omnibus providere interea, donec Magister novus electus fuerit et admissus.

CAP. 9
De qualitate novi Magistri eligendi

Caput caeteris membris congruum esse, eisdemque providere et opem ferre diligenter oportet. Volumus idcirco et statuimus, ut Magister collegii praedicti eligendus sit natione Anglus, et quem socii vel certis argumentis vel longa experientia persuasi crediderint omni fidelitate, industria, studio, et bona conscientia rem domesticam prudenter administraturum, statuta nostra observaturum, bona, terras, possessiones, libertates, privilegia, et ius unumquodque collegii pro viribus suis defensurum. Volumus etiam ut nemo in Magistrum eligatur, nisi qui octo annos integros sacrae theologiae studium publice sit professus, et pro tali professore vulgo sit habitus, quique etiam verbum Domini publice praedicaverit, et concionatoris munus saepius obiverit, qui sit in ministrorum ordinem cooptatus, quique Papismum, haereses, superstitiones, et errores omnes ex animo abhorret et detestatur: qui denique in rebus suis, et iis quae sibi ab aliis aliquando commissae fuerint, virum diligentem, frugi, et probum se gesserit, et cuius opinio apud bonos viros non sit imminuta aut gravata, et qui ad annum trigesimum aetatis suae pervenerit, et per sexdecim annos in universitate Cantabrigiae in literarum studiis diligenter versatus sit. Talis si quis reperiatur inter collegii socios, eundem in Domino praecipimus eligendum. Sin minus, eiusmodi quaeratur eorum qui aliquando fuerunt eiusdem collegii socii. Quod si neque apud illos talis idoneus reperiri queat, tum ex collegio Christi (quod caeteris praeponi volumus) et eo deficiente, ex tota Cantabrigiae universitate licebit eligere, dummodo qualitatibus ac donis antea requisitis praeclare ornatus fuerit.

CAP. 10
De antecedentibus electionem Magistri

Ut Magistri electio et incorrupta et legitima esse possit, quemadmodum nos omni modo cupimus, proinde socios ad quos huius electionis ius pertinet, tria haec praestare integerrime volumus antequam ad eligendum Magistrum accesserint. Primum ut conscientiam afferant liberam, sinceram, nulla gratia aut alia affectione impeditam, quominus eum eligant, quem bonorum omnium iudiciis simpliciter dignissimum esse constabit. Qua in re tantam ab illis fidem et curam requirimus, quantam cogitare maximam licet. Deinde ut nulli suum suffragium ullo modo promittant, aut pactiones ullas vel apertas vel occultas faciant: sed suum iudicium ad tempus electionis liberrimum reservent. Postremo quoniam singulis potestatem damus nominandi quos sciverint dignos esse hoc Magistratu (dummodo id fecerint tribus ante electionem diebus) ut eiusmodi virum semper nominent, qui est omnibus illis donis praeditus quae in superiore Statuto requiruntur. Quod si quis contra fecerit, aut indignum aliquem, id est, virum illis non ornatum nominaverit, iudicio maioris partis sociorum stipendio caeterisque societatis suae emolumentis (praeter communias hebdomadarias) per integri anni spatium privabitur. Quod si quis ullo modo suffragium venale fecerit, vel in electione Magistri, vel in ulla alia concessione nomine collegii fienda, hunc ipso facto e collegio amotum volumus. Et quo magis libere socii suffragia sua dent in electione Magistri, volumus et statuimus, ut si in gratiam et favorem cuiusquam literae, vel nuncius a quacunque persona ad socios seu eorum aliquem mittantur vel destinentur, aut petitio cuiusquam intervenerit, tunc is inhabilis ad capessendum locum Magistri omnino reputetur, et electio de ipso facto prorsus nulla et irrita habeatur.

CAP. II

De modo et forma eligendi Magistri

Porro ne hoc corpus principali suo membro aliquando careat diutius, quam par est, volumus et statuimus, ut durante vita nostra, is magister, socius, et scholaris collegii praedicti sit, quem vel quos nos designabimus et admittemus. Postquam vero ex hac vita migraverimus, electionem fieri ad formam sequentem ordinamus. Primum senior socius iuxta admissionem inter eos qui tum domi praesentes erunt, illis una convocatis rem aperiat et vacationem officii Magistri (quamprimum illud cognoverit) absque omni mora notam faciat, atque de die et hora electionis futurae palam et diligenter admoneat. Quod si qui sociorum absentes fuerint, illorum adventus per septem tantum dies immediate sequentes expectabitur. Atque ut illis absentibus haec Magistri vacatio facilius innotescat, schedula de die et hora futurae electionis per eundem seniorem socium ostio sacelli per hos septem dies continuo affigetur, nec ullo alio modo absentes de futura electione admoneri volumus.

Die igitur septimo post agnitam vacationem, mane hora quinta eiusdem diei, tam socii, quam scholares omnes, ac pensionarii congregabuntur in sacello praedicto, ubi primum preces ordinariae offerentur Deo, deinde concio habebitur vel ab ipso seniore socio (si voluerit) vel ad eius mandatum ab aliquo alio sociorum tum praesentium, dummodo de hoc officio antea per quinque dies ad minimum admoneatur. In hac autem concione socios hortabitur ad eligendum talem virum in Magistrum, qualem statuta nostra descripserint et collegii status iure postulare videbitur. Postea Eucharistia, id est, coena Domini celebrabitur, cuius omnes socios, scholares, pensionarios, caeterosque inhabitantes participes esse volumus. Finitis autem his omnibus pietatis et religionis exercitiis, quibus electores ad debitum officium alacrius et religiosius praestandum excitentur, praedictus senior (caeteris omnibus praeter socios prius exclusis) palam leget statuta nostra de qualitate Magistri eligendi: quibus lectis socius praedictus associet sibi duos alios socios maxime seniores praesentium iuxta admissionem, qui acceptis singulorum suffragiis omnia fideliter tractabunt, quae ad perficiendum electionem pertinent: quae ut fidelius faciant illi, primum inspectis et tactis sacrosanctis Christi Evangeliis singillatim iurabunt in hunc modum. Ego N.T. Deum testor in conscientia mea me in hac electione statuta nuper lecta fideliter et integre observasse et observaturum: et illum in Magistrum electurum, quem his statutis nuper lectis significari et apertius describi mea conscientia iudicabit, omni illegitima affectione, metu, odio, amore et similibus sepositis. Quod ipsum iuramentum reliqui omnes socii praestabunt, unus post alterum, servato ordine senioritatis suae. Quam etiam iuramenti formam et nullam aliam ante electionem Magistri semper observari volumus.

Praestito hoc iuramento, senior antedictus coram duobus sociis aliis suffragium suum propria manu scribet: postea alii duo sua similiter suffragia scribent. Postremo omnes alii socii praesentes sua suffragia coram praedictis tribus senioribus quiete deponent, et scribent propriis ipsorum manibus. Omnes autem hac aut simili forma scribent. Ego N.T. eligo in Magistrum huius collegii N.N. etc. Quae omnia suffragia ita conscripta praefatus senior vel alius quispiam illorum trium aperte et distincte legat coram omnibus sociis praesentibus, et in quem maior pars praesentium consenserint, ille pro electo habeatur absque contradictione cuiuscunque. Quam electionem dictus senior, antequam recedat, sub hac forma pronunciare tenebitur. Ego N.T. senior huius collegii socius nomine meo, et nomine omnium sociorum, seu maioris partis eorundem, electum vobis pronuntio N.N. in Magistrum huius collegii. Quod si nec primo, nec secundo scrutinio maior pars sociorum in unam personam consentire queat, tunc compromittant omnes et singuli socii praesentes sua suffragia quinque vel, si quatuor tantum socii fuerint, tribus sociis senioribus omnium praesentium: et in quem maior pars ipsorum seniorum consenserit, pro electo habeatur absque haesitatione et contradictione quacunque. Hos autem seniores arctamus sub poena amissionis societatum suarum ipso facto ut electionem ibidem perficiant ante horam duodecimam eiusdem diei: quam electionem praefatus senior aut (illo in Magistrum electo) qui senioritate proximus est, sub poena manifesti periurii et perpetuae expulsionis e collegio teneatur pronunciare, et personam sic electam admittere (si in oppido fuerit) sin minus, quam primum venire poterit; cuius adventum dictus senior omni diligentia procurabit.

Electus autem Magister hoc iuramentum praestabit, quod sequitur. Ego N.T. Deum testor, me veram Christi religionem, Papismo et caeteris haeresibus contrariam, ex animo complexurum: scripturae authoritatem vel optimorum hominum iudiciis praepositurum: caetera quae ex verbo Dei nulla ratione probari possint pro humanis habiturum: authoritatem Regiam in hominibus eius dominationis summam, et externorum Episcoporum et Principum et potestatum quarumcumque iurisdictioni minime subiectam aestimaturum: opiniones verbo Dei contrarias, omnesque haereses omni diligentia refutaturum, denique vera consuetis, scripta non scriptis in causa religionis semper ante-habiturum. Secundo eundem Deum testor in Christo Jesu, atque fideliter promitto, me collegium hoc cuius nunc sum electus Magister omni cura et diligentia administraturum, omniaque illius bona, terras, tenementa, possessiones, redditus, libertates, iura, privilegia, caeteras-que res universas tam mobiles quam immobiles integre conservaturum: statuta omnia et ordinationes huius collegii, quae et ad dei gloriam, et ad collegii decus ac emolumentum spectare scivero (quantum in me est) inviolate observaturum, et ab aliis observari curaturum, omnique personarum exceptione posthabita, neque dispensationem aliquam adversus eadem statuta aut eorum aliquod impetrabo, nec ab aliis curabo impetrari, nec impetratam acceptabo ullo modo. Haec omnia in me recipio, et hoc iureiurando polliceor (quatenus Statutis regni editis aut edendis non repugnent) sicut me Deus adiuvet in Christo Jesu.

His autem peractis volumus et statuimus, ut praenominatus senior socius (cui tempore vacationis omnium rerum administratio et custodia concedebatur) vel, illo electo, socius senior proximus, statim post hoc iuramentum, Magistro nuper electo verum et integrum praebeat computum de rebus collegii universis per se custoditis et administratis: thesaurum universum, librum statutorum, claves cistarum quae ad illius officium pertinent, omnia ornamenta, scriptaque universa, et munimenta quaecunque ad dictum collegium pertinentia illi aperiat, ac tradat iuxta tenorem nostrorum statutorum custodienda: idque in praesentia omnium sociorum domi praesentium; de quibus universis Magister ipse intra quatuor dies novum conficiet inventorium, quod a sociis omnibus lectum et approbatum intra collegii Thesaurarium recondetur.

CAP. 12

De subsequentibus electionem

Electo et pronunciato novo Magistro, mox socii duo seniores (caeteris etiam omnibus per eosdem convocatis) electionem praedicti Magistri Procancellario universitatis seu vices ipsius gerenti significabunt.

CAP. 13

De Magistri (si res exigat) amotione

Curandum est praeterea, ut non solum idoneus quispiam in Magistrum eligatur, sed etiam (si forte idem aberraverit) mox aut reformetur aut Magistratum suum abdicare cogatur. Statuimus igitur, quod si quis Magister negligens fuerit in administratione sua, et in his quae ad ipsius officium pertinent, aut de inhonesta conversatione et vitae incontinentia vehementer suspectus, semel per Magistrum collegii Christi et duos seniores doctores Theologiae, aut eorum defectu, duos Baccalaureos in eadem Academia seniores admoneatur, atque iterato (si opus fuerit) et si secundo admonitus non illico sese emendaverit, sive de haeresi, de laesa majestate, de simonia, de usura, de periurio coram iudice commisso, de furto notabili, de homicidio voluntario, de incestu, adulterio, seu fornicatione manifestis, de dilapidatione alienationeve terrarum, tenementorum, reddituum, aut distractione illicita bonorum aut rerum ipsius collegii, aut ullo alio consimili crimine coram praedicto Magistro, et duobus in sacra Theologia Doctoribus maxime senioribus in Academia praesentibus, sive, ob eorum defectum, Baccalaureis in eadem senioribus, evidenti probatione convictus fuerit: tum per praedictum Magistrum, cum assensu aliorum Doctorum aut Baccalaureorum, magistratu privetur et omni eius emolumento. Volumus etiam et statuimus, si Magistrum ad ecclesiasticum aliquod beneficium curam animarum habens annexam promoveri contigerit, locum ipsius in collegio praedicto a tempore inductionis suae in beneficium praedictum, vel corporalis possessionis, aut perceptionis fructum eiusdem ipso facto

vacare: sociisque collegii praedicti alium Magistrum eius loco eligendi
iuxta formam antea praescriptam, liberam damus facultatem.

CAP. 14
De Decano sive catechista

De Magistro hactenus statutum est, cui, ne nimio onere prematur,
Decanum sive Catechistam supponimus, qui primo die Octobris, vel
(si ille dies dominicus sit) secundo, per Magistrum, sive eius locum
tenentem, et maiorem partem sociorum, ex iisdem sociis eligatur. Cuius
officium erit singulis annis intra tres dies a magno totius anni computo
statuta collegii sociis et scholaribus omnibus tunc praesentibus legere,
et quaque hebdomada uniuscuiusque termini intra collegii sacellum
unicam audire disputationem in Theologia die veneris duarum horarum
spatio, a quarta, videlicet, ad sextam nisi festi solennitas impediat: et
ex eius arbitrio atque moderatione cuique spatium limitabitur posi-
tionem suam pronuntiandi, argumentandi, et replicandi, aut brevius aut
prolixius. Eundem etiam volumus sociorum suorum in divinis officiis
celebrandis negligentias annotare, absentiae cuiusque aut tarditatis
causam legitime approbare, delinquentes in praemissis mulctare
monitoresque duos e discipulis constituere, qui caeterorum discipulorum tarditates, absentias et neglectus (tam quoad divina officia
celebranda, quam quoad scholastica exercitamenta forinseca) in
quibusdam schedulis inscribent, quas Decanus ipse singulis diebus
veneris cuiusque hebdomadae proponet legendas: singulis denique
hebdomadis die Sabbathi hora tertia post meridiem unius horae spatio
aliquem articulum religionis Christianae explicabit et docebit, et
scholares, pensionarios omnesque inhabitantes in collegio pro arbitrio
et prudentia sua examinabit ut singulorum profectum melius cognoscat:
reliquos etiam socios volumus, ut huic in istorum omnium examinatione
opem ferant quoties opus erit iudicio Magistri et maioris partis sociorum. Decanus vero pro stipendio accipiet quinquaginta tres solidos et
quatuor denarios annuatim.

CAP. 15
De mulctis per Decanum cuique imponendis

Et ne quem severius, quam par est, puniat, eundem hoc moderamine
uti volumus quoad divina officia et Theologica exercitia; primum

socium quemque pro unaquaque tarditate mulctabit obolo, pro quaque absentia denario unico, pro neglecto cursu et ordine in precibus, denariis duodecem. Quoad domesticas disputationes, socii cuiusque tarditas denario mulctabitur, absentia denariis quatuor, neglectus ordo sex solidis et octo denariis: discipulus quisque pro sua tarditate in eisdem divinis obolo, pro absentia vero denario. In scholasticis vero exercitamentis et domesticis et forensibus (utpote sophismatibus pomeridianis in scholis publicis, sive ante meridiem in sermonibus ad clerum) pro quaque tarditate quadrante, pro absentia obolo: pro neglecto cursu duodecim denariis, si adultus, alioqui virga corrigatur. Tarditatem intelligimus in disputationibus post respondentis expositam sententiam, in divinis officiis post primum psalmum. Adjicimus quod si quis sociorum ordinem et cursum suum non servaverit, tunc qui proximus illi in ordine fuerit, illius supplebit negligentiam, et delinquens nihilominus hebdomada proxima parem illi vicissim referet gratiam: alioqui ipse mulctabitur iterato: mulctarum postremo illarum emolumentum in usum convictus sociorum cedere volumus. Ad quas levandas, simulque reprimendas quorundam (si quae fuerint) obstinatas arrogantias, magistrum ei adiutorem esse iubemus, et roboris praebitorem, quod a capite membra suscipere debent.

CAP. 16
De Senescallo

Post Decanum proximo loco est Senescallus, qui a Magistro, sociis, scholaribus et pensionariis tantum pecuniae prae manu singulis mensibus accipiat quantum in sumptum communiarum cuiusque eorum sufficiat: id vero Magister, habita ratione eius summae quae vulgariter in singulos menses soleat sufficere, moderabitur; ex ea pecunia procurabit Senescallus victualia, quae singulis hebdomadis erunt necessaria comparari. Quod erit expositum, et ad quam summam communiae praedictae ascendent, libello per se vel per mancipem describet, rationemque hebdomadatim Magistro vel eius locum tenenti et sociis praesentibus die Sabbathi a prandio idem Senescallus aut manceps fideliter reddet. Nemo sociorum absit ab hoc computo absque Magistri aut eius locum tenentis licentia, sub poena duorum denariorum.

CAP. 17
De Sociorum qualitate

De Magistro, Decano et Senescallo antea statutum est: sequitur ut de sociis tanquam de potioribus et solidioribus membris pari ratione decernamus. Socios igitur eligi volumus, Anglos, ex collegii scholaribus, qui vel magistri in artibus sunt, vel saltem Baccalaurei tertii anni: et qui pauperiores adiutores habuerint, et egent magis, illos semper in quaque electione praeferendos esse statuimus: ob quod atque ob caetera quae nos movent, comitatus Essexiae et Northamtoniae caeteris omnibus praeponendos esse decrevimus: ita tamen ut non sint plures ex uno comitatu antedictorum praeter unum: quod de singulis aliis comitatibus totius regni observari volumus: neque plures quam unum ex ullo alio comitatu totius Angliae socios in collegio nostro praedicto esse permittimus unquam: oppida omnia et civitates quibuscunque privilegiis exempta fuerint, ad illum tamen comitatum pertinere intelligimus, intra cuius fines situantur. Verum si nulli ex collegii Scholaribus idonei reperiantur, ex aliis studiosis intra collegium eligere licebit: semper tamen ex egentioribus probioribus et doctioribus. Statuimus enim ut qui valde pauperes sint, nec ullos habent adiutores, quorum liberalitate vitam in Academia degant, in omni electione soli eligantur. Non est enim aequum, ut quae nos pauperibus tantum dicavimus, ad divites aut ad eos qui commode et moderate aliunde absque societate vivere possint, aliquando transferantur. Eiusmodi ergo ne nominari in Electione quidem volumus, neque a magistro neque a sociorum aliquo, sub poena amittendi semestris stipendii. Hos igitur pauperes, sive ex collegio, sive ex Academia fuerint (acto prius anno vigesimo primo) eligi volumus: peritos etiam esse volumus, primum in his tribus linguis, Graeca, Latina, et Hebraea, ita ut illas intelligere possint: deinde in Rhetorica, Dialectica, Physica, quarum artium praecepta et vere scire, et in usum ac praxin reducere apti sunto: ante omnia vero purae religionis, Papismo et caeteris haeresibus contrariae, professores erunt, quique vitam moresque secundum eam conformaverint: Quae omnia cum non cito comparari possint, neminem in socium admitti volumus, qui non sex ad minimum integris annis studuerit in Academia Cantabrigiensi.

CAP. 18
De antecedentibus electionem

Nunc vero quo facilius sociorum nostrorum loci et ornamenta viris
eruditis et hisce qualitatibus praeditis tantum tribuantur, et qui indigni
sunt (utpote iisdem destituti) perpetuo arceantur, statuimus et ordinamus, ut Magister, convocatis sociis, illos admoneat quinque dies ante
diem electionis futurae, quotiescunque locus alicuius socii vacabit
(vacare autem nolumus ultra spatium ad summum unius mensis): in
quibus quinque diebus Magister sociique debent diligenter inquirere de
eorum religione, paupertate, doctrina et moribus, qui ab illis nominati
erunt in electionem futuram. Licebit enim Magistro et cuique sociorum
nominare quemcunque qui sua ipsorum conscientia coram Deo
iudicabitur dignus, qui eligatur in proxima electione futura: ita tamen
ut id faciant quarto die ante electionem. Quo die volumus eligendorum
nomina in schedula scripta a quovis nominante ad Magistrum deferri,
quo illa tuto ac fideliter apud se custodiat usque in diem electionis. Ergo
quicunque non erunt hoc modo et die nominati, non erunt eodem
tempore eligibiles. Quae res quia maximi momenti est, tam Magistro
quam sociis interdicimus, ne indignum aliquem, id est, non omnibus
qualitatibus saltem mediocriter ornatum, eligendum nominent, sub
poena amissionis annui stipendii, quod in collegii commodum cedet.

Atque ne Magister aut socius quispiam fallatur ignoratione nominatorum, aut falsis hominum de illis testimoniis, decernimus, ut Magister
convocatis ad se sociis in aliquo opportuno collegii loco (ut in aula vel
sacello, vel si occasio postulat, in cubiculo suo) ita tamen ut alii studiosi
intersint, si velint, nec ulli, qui est in collegio, interesse prohibeatur.
Hoc modo atque ibidem publice nominatos tribus ante electionem
diebus examinari curet. Ac primum duos ex sociis, quos ad hanc
provinciam obeundam maxime idoneos pro illo tempore iudicabit,
examinatores constituet, qui ita constituti nullis aliis collegii exercitiis,
durante electionis tempore, astringentur; sed tantum ad examinandum
et probandum ipsos nominatos se parabunt: ideoque tribus illis exa-
minationis diebus interesse tenebuntur ad praestandum officium suum.
Tempus examinandi erit ab hora octava matutina usque ad horam
decimam, nisi aliter iustis de causis Magistro et maiori parti sociorum
visum fuerit tempus illud abbreviare, aut propter negotia collegii
magis necessaria in tempus pomeridianum transferre: ita tamen ut duae
saltem horae singulis quibusque diebus in examinatione insumantur.

Examinatores igitur primo die periculum facient in lingua Graeca et Hebraea, secundo in Rhetorica et Logica, tertio vero in Physica. Quo etiam die Catechista, aut locum eius tenens, ad mandatum Magistri periculum faciet (si opus sit) in Theologia et vera cognitione Dei. Neque vero examinandi munus his sociis ita astringi volumus, ut nemini praeterea examinare et opponere liceat: quin et Magistro et sociorum cuilibet examinandi libertatem concedimus pro arbitrio, dummodo omnia ordine et decore fiant. Illud autem Magistrum attingit videre ut religiose observetur. Finita autem examinatione, et probe cognitis nominatorum religione, moribus et doctrina, Magister et socii sese parabunt ad electionem in hunc modum sequente capite descriptum.

CAP. 19
De sociorum electione

Ea est corporis politici ratio, ut, nisi veteribus nova membra succedant, totius interitus paulatim sequatur: idcirco decrevimus, quoties aliquis sociorum e societate sua quacunque de causa decesserit intra quatuor hebdomadas immediate sequentes novam electionem fieri: nisi status collegii propter aliquod insigne detrimentum impedierit: quo tantum casu permittimus electionem differri, quousque secundum iudicium Magistri et maioris partis sociorum idem damnum possit plenarie resarciri. Veruntamen tam Magistri, quam sociorum conscientias oneramus in Domino, ut illud restitui, quam cito poterit, omni diligentia curent: postquam vero restituatur, absque omni mora ac dilatione ad novam procedatur electionem, quae in hunc modum fiet. Magister et socii convenient omnes hora et loco per Magistrum assignatis intra collegium; in quorum praesentia senior socius praesentium distincte leget statuta de sociorum qualitate, de antecedentibus electionem, atque de ipsorum sociorum electione; et quo magis libere Magister et socii suffragia sua dent in electione sociorum vel scholarium, volumus et statuimus quod si in gratiam vel favorem alicuius literae vel nuncius a quacunque persona ad Magistrum et socios seu eorum aliquem mittantur, aut destinentur, tunc is inhabilis ad capessendum locum socii vel scholaris omnino reputetur, et electio de ipso facto prorsus irrita et nulla habeatur. Volumus etiam et statuimus, ut nullus ex sociis seu scholaribus praedictis resignationem aut abdicationem iuris sui nisi simplicem et absolutam faciet. Quod si quis resignaverit aut abdicaverit locum suum sub conditione certae personae eligendae

vel sub alia conditione quacunque, resignationem huiusmodi pro
simplici haberi volumus, et ab eo tempore locum eius vacare decernimus, ac si simpliciter et absolute resignasset aut abdicasset. Qui vero
pecuniam dederit cuiquam pro resignatione sua et abdicatione praedicta vel pro suffragio, aut etiam pactus est se daturum, inhabilis
reputetur, et qui sic acceperit, iure societatis aut scholariatus de-
privetur.

Deinde lectis statutis praedictis, Magister primum, deinde reliqui per
ordinem senioritatis suae, tactis Christi Evangeliis, hoc iusiurandum
praestent: Ego N.T. Deum testor in conscientia mea me in hac electione
statuta nuper lecta fideliter et integre observasse et observaturum, et
illum in socium futurum electurum quem haec statuta nuper lecta
significare et apertius describere conscientia mea iudicabit, omni
illegitima affectione, metu, odio, amore et similibus sepositis. Quod
ipsum iuramentum reliqui omnes socii praestabunt, unus post alterum
servato ordine senioritatis suae: quam etiam iuramenti formam, et
nullam aliam ante sociorum electionem observari volumus. Praestito
hoc iuramento, Magister et duo seniores socii praesentium stabunt in
sacello collegii, aut in aliquo alio loco qui Magistro in hanc rem op-
portunus videbitur: tum Magister et dicti seniores scribent sua suffragia
manibus propriis sub hac vel consimili forma: Ego N. eligo N.T. in
socium huius collegii. Deinde singuli socii praesentes suffragia sua
similiter scribent singulatim: et in quem vel quos maior pars suffra-
giorum totius numeri ex Magistro et sociis consenserit, pro electo
habeatur. Quod ita intelligi volumus, ut Magister unicum suffragium,
idque tantum affirmativum habeat. Quem sic electum teneatur pronunciare et admittere. Quod si suffragia Magistri et sociorum in duas
vel plures partes dividantur, ita ut maior pars praesentium in aliquem
convenire nequeat, tunc in quem Magister cum sociis medietatem
facientes praesentium omnium consenserint, pro electo habeatur absque
haesitatione vel contradictione aliqua: cuius electio per Magistrum
nomine maioris partis praesentium pronuncietur. Nam in hoc casu et
similibus, quoties continget vel in sociorum vel scholarium electionibus,
sive in ullis aliis concessionibus, Magistrum et socios in duas aequales
partes dividi, tum semper Magistri suffragium (nunquam enim illi vocem
negativam concedimus) pro duobus suffragiis computari decernimus
tenore praesentis statuti.

Qui sic electus diligenter perlegat omnia statuta nostra, quae pro
administrando hoc collegio edidimus, ne propter illorum ignorantiam

assumat Dei nomen in vanum. Quam ob causam concedetur illi usus
exemplaris libri statutorum, quousque illum perlegerit. Deinde praesentetur coram societate, et iuret se observaturum statuta omnia huius
collegii, ad hunc qui sequitur modum: Ego N.T. Deum testor me
veram Christi religionem, Papismo et caeteris omnibus haeresibus
contrariam, amplexurum, atque in vim pacti promitto me veraciter
atque integre observaturum statuta omnia et singula quae Gualtherus
Mildmaius fundator huius collegii pro eodem administrando per se
ediderit, et curabo, quantum in me fuerit, a consociis meis idem fieri:
Magistro sive eius locum tenenti in omnibus parebo quaecunque legitime imperaverit: consilia eiusdem collegii secreta (quoad iuste licuerit)
nemini pandam: nihil in quo eidem collegio commodi aut honoris
accessio aliqua fieri possit, impediam, sed magis pro meis viribus pro-
curabo: nemini sociorum consentiam, ut ad facultatem aliam se divertat
pro gradu in ea suscipiendo, praeterquam ad Theologiae duntaxat:
nullam ullo tempore adversus aliquod statutorum fundatoris nostri,
sive adversus hoc iuramentum meum dispensationem impetrabo nec
curabo impetrari, nec ab aliis impetratam acceptabo ullo modo: haec
omnia in me recipio, et hoc iureiurando polliceor, quatenus statutis
regni editis aut edendis non repugnent, sicut me Deus adjuvet per
Christum Jesum. His omnibus ita peractis secundum statuta nostra,
Magister, brevi exhortatione prius habita ad electum vel electos, hac
illos forma in societatem admittet: Ego N.N. Magister huius collegii
admitto te in socium eiusdem, in nomine Patris et Filii et Spiritus
sancti. Amen.

CAP. 20
De cultu Dei

Tria sunt quae socios huius Collegii omnes imprimis curare cupimus:
Dei scilicet cultus, fidei incrementum, et morum probitas: quoad Dei
cultum, principio hoc statuimus, quod singulis diebus, praecipue vero
Dominicis, socii omnes, scholares, pensionarii, caeterique inhabitantes,
publicis precibus aderunt horis congruis per Magistrum sive eius locum
tenentem assignandis: quibus et Magistrum ipsum interesse volumus,
si non legitime impediatur. Idemque cuiusque termini initio ad minimum ad socios et scholares eiusdem collegii sacello publice coeuntes
sacram concionem habebit in propria persona, et una etiam sacram
Eucharistiam eodem tempore administrabit; ut autem utrumque saepius
faciat, in Domino adhortamur.

CAP. 21
De sociorum exercitamento, studiis, et ordine

Quod attinet ad fidei incrementum (cui secundum locum dedimus) omnes in hoc collegium admittendos, sive illi socii fuerint, sive scholares, sive etiam pensionarii, admonitos esse volumus, nos unum hunc nobis scopum in hoc collegio erigendo proposuisse, ut quam plurimos ad sacrum verbi divini et sacramentorum ministerium idoneos redderemus: ut ex hoc seminario haberet Anglicana ecclesia, quos ad erudiendum populum pastorumque munus subeundum (rem ex omnibus maxime necessariam) evocare possit. Sciant itaque socii et scholares, qui alio consilio se collegio obtrudent, quam ut sacrae Theologiae se addicant, tandemque in verbo praedicando laborent, se spem nostram frustrari, locumque socii aut scholaris praeter institutum nostrum occupare: quam rem serio eos admonemus uti diligenter curent, scituros se aliquando fraudis per eos admissae reddituros Domino rationem. Et ne totum tamen hoc quicquid est oneris, eorum nudis permittamus conscientiis (quanquam philosophiae caeterisque artibus eos erudiri cupimus, moremque Academiae in ea reservari volumus, tam in lectionibus audiendis quam in aliis exercitiis, ac etiam in gradibus qui artium proprii sunt suscipiendis) statuimus tamen, ut socii collegii praedicti singulis hebdomadis unicam habeant in Sacra Theologia disputationem, in qua quisque suo ordine erit respondens, opponentes vero duo erunt; quem locum etiam quisque ex sociis suo ordine obibunt, iuxta morem in caeteris collegiis usitatum: et quia videmus nihil de toto hoc genere Scholastici in Sacra Theologia exercitii posse in universum praescribi, quod vel instituto nostro plene sit satisfacturum, vel non incurret in aliquam difficultatem, propterea liberam facimus potestatem Magistro collegii praedicti, cum consensu maioris partis sociorum, quam uberiorem exercitiorum rationem, et ad promovendum studium theologiae, formandosque verbi ministros statuent esse commodissimam, pro temporum ratione praescribendi: quod vero erit praescriptum, id a sociis omnibus sub poenis aliorum exercitiorum nomine designatis, volumus observari. Ex toto autem sociorum dicti collegii numero quatuor maxime seniores ad minimum verbi et sacramentorum ministros esse volumus, et ad eum ordinem admitti intra annum unum a die publicationis statutorum nostrorum in collegio praedicto: ut autem quisque eorum ministrorum e collegio discesserit, ita proximum ex sociis iuxta ordinem senioritatis suae intra sex menses a tempore recessus dicti ministri a collegio praedicto ad ordinem ministri verbi et sacramentorum promoveri volumus: sic ut non pauciores quam quatuor ministri semper sint in collegio praedicto. Et qui ad hoc praescriptum non erit verbi et sacramentorum minister, ius societatis suae in perpetuum amittat. Qui vero erunt ad hunc gradum sacri ministerii vocati, ii sciant nos prae caeteris in eorum prudentia et cura, ut quam optimis institutis reliqui imbuantur formenturque in Christo, plurimum fiduciae posuisse: rogamusque in Domino ut tanquam pro grege sibi commisso diligenter sibi vigilandum esse statuant.

In mensa singulis prandiis Biblia ante et post prandium et coenam omnes diligenter audiant et attente, donec Magister aut eius locum tenens bibliarium finire iusserit. De sermone Latino in privatis et familiaribus congressibus retinendo, Magistri iudicio esse permittimus, quid in ea re censeat esse praescribendum; ita tamen ut illo omnes utantur, quemadmodum illis utile futurum Magister ipse iudicabit.

CAP. 22
De moribus improbis, vetitis cuique socio

Sed quia parum iuvat doctos esse nisi boni sint, idcirco volumus et statuimus, quod nemo sociorum eorundem tabernas publicas, domos suspectas, aut locum aliquem inhonestum frequentet; nemo compotationes, ingurgitationes, aut armorum gestationes exerceat; nemo cum mulieribus colloquio secreto alicubi utatur, praesertim intra cameras aliquas dicti collegii, quas foeminam nullam (si sola sit) aliquando ingredi aut in eisdem manere volumus, praeterquam aegrotationis tempore, Magistro aut eius locum tenenti cognite et approbate. Nemo praeterea sit nocturnus deambulator, aut per noctem foris extra dictum collegium cubet aliquo loco intra millia passuum tria a collegio eodem, aut esse omnino audeat extra collegii ipsius ambitum, ultra nonam alicuius noctis horam, a festo divi Michaelis ad festum usque Paschae, seu decimam horam a festo Paschae ad festum usque Divi Michaelis, nisi ex causa necessaria per Magistrum sive eius locum tenentem approbanda. Nemo ad haec canes aut rapaces aves nutriat, tesserisve, alea, aut chartis ludat, ne remittendi quidem animi gratia. Nemo denique seniorem suum contemnat; sed tam domi quam foris, in sacello et mensa, in scholis et vicis illi cedat, nisi forte gradu aliquo scholastico fuerit superior: nam nisi gradus impediat, seniorem quemque suum iuniorem praeire semper volumus omnibus in locis.

CAP. 23
De stipendio, et emolumentis sociorum

Et quoniam boni bene merentur, et digni sunt praemio, idcirco volumus et statuimus, quod quisque praedictorum ministrorum singulis annis ad tempora consuetudinaria pro stipendio suo recipiat triginta solidos per manum Magistri seu locum eius tenentis integre persolvendos. Volumus praeterea singulis hebdomadis pro uniuscuiusque socii communiis, senescallo duos solidos tradi, quam summam (si fieri possit) communiae non excedant: veruntamen si excesserint aliquando, residuum quisque persolvet ex pecunia sua, recepturus quod superest, si quando fuerint minores: pro vestitura autem annua viginti sex solidos et octo denarios: sumptus panis et vini aliarumque rerum ad Eucharistiam celebrandam et preces communes necessariarum ex publico collegii aerario persolvet: si vero quisquam ex sociis minister non fuerit, illum communiis et vestitura antedictis contentum esse volumus, nec ultra quicquam ex supradictis recipere, quoad ille ad sacrum ministerium admittatur.

CAP. 24
Quantum aliunde eis recipere liceat

Si quis sociorum substantiam annuam assecutus fuerit, unde possit commode sustentari, non est iustum ut ille stipendia pauperibus et egenis deputata suscipiat: idcirco volumus et statuimus, quod si quisquam sociorum assecutus fuerit patrimonium, liberam capellam, pensionem, seu beneficium simplex, quod valorem annuum decem librarum excedat, tunc post alicuius eorundem pacificam possessionem desinat ipso facto pro socio haberi. Si quis ex sociis praedicti collegii ad beneficium cuiuscunque valoris curam animarum habens annexam admissus fuerit et institutus, simul atque in possessionem eiusdem beneficii fuerit inductus, et pacificam possessionem fuerit assecutus, vel per eum steterit, quominus inducatur, vel pacificam possessionem adipiscatur, locum ipsius in collegio praedicto volumus vacare ipso facto, ita ut deinceps pro socio eiusdem collegii minime habeatur aut reputetur.

CAP. 25
De prandendi et coenandi loco

Et quoniam eos omnes in unitatem quandam integrari cupimus, ut sint tanquam corpus unum sub Magistro, totius collegii capite: idcirco omnes socios, scholares et pensionarios collegii praedicti in publica eius aula prandere et coenare volumus, nec quenquam eorum seorsim in cubiculis vel aliis locis intra collegium prandium vel coenam habere permittimus: nisi ex causa rationabili, Magistri seu eius locum tenentis iudicio approbanda. Et quanquam alibi statuerimus absentem socium neminem communias suas habiturum: volumus tamen, si pestis aut infectio ulla contagiosa intra collegium, aut Parochiam in qua dictum collegium situatur, orta fuerit, sive alibi intra universitatem Cantabrigiae, adeo ut magnus et insignis scholarium numerus illinc ob eandem contagionem egressus fuerit, tunc Magistro et sociis licebit in aliquem alium locum se conferre, ubi commodius pro eis provideri possit, iuxta impensas, quas eidem domi fecissent. Volumus etiam, quod si quis eorum aegrotet, aut credibiliter de pestis infectione suspectus fuerit, ut commode inter sanos versari nequiverit, idque Magistro constiterit et maiori parti sociorum: tunc eorum concessione locum aliquem idoneum sibi petet, ubi prandere possit, et emolumenta praedicta suscipere, pro stipendio, viz., communiis et vestitura, ac si praesens esset intra collegium.

CAP. 26
Quamdiu sociis abesse a collegio dicto licuerit

Urgent plerumque negotia unumquemque, ut aliquando longius egredi a dicto collegio necesse sit; atque ob eam rem statuimus, quod singulis annis unusquisque sociorum dies habeat pro arbitrio viginti lusorios, quibus abesse poterit a dicto collegio, modo id ante a Magistro sive eius locum tenente sibi licere petierit, et ea quae decuit reverentia. Quod si tam urgens erit eius causa, ut Magister praedictus sive eius locum tenens in conscientia sua et coram Deo necessariam approbaverit: tunc eidem amplius concedere posse volumus dies alios triginta intra eundem annum, aut simul aut seorsim. Et praeter haec, si vel alia causa supervenerit, aut eadem institerit vehementius, quae Magistro dicto aut eius locum tenenti et maiori parti sociorum secundum Deum et eorum conscientias iusta videbitur, tunc iterum per Magistri sive eius locum tenentis concessionem idem socius se possit absentare per alios intra eundem annum triginta dies. Caeterum si praeter haec tempora et dies istos limitatos intra unius anni spatium quispiam diutius se absentaverit (nisi ingenti aegrotatione aut detentione violenta, quae per Magistrum et maiorem partem sociorum approbabitur) quo minus intra dictos dies redierit, illum deinceps omni iure societatis privari volumus in collegio dicto. Quod si quispiam sociorum legitime abfuerit, cuius tamen reditus ad commodum et honorem collegii eiusdem Magistro sive eius locum tenenti et maiori parti sociorum videbitur necessarius, ille, si revocatus non illico redierit, et quamprimum congrue potuerit nisi iustam reddiderit causam eisdem probandam societate item sua sit privatus. Ita etiam licentiam illam sociis concedendam moderari volumus, ut uno simul tempore non ultra tertiam partem sociorum absint. Atque etiam universo illo tempore quo sint absentes (nisi in casibus superiore statuto nominatis) illorum nemini quicquam pro communiis suis allocabitur de bonis ipsius collegii, sed communiae absentis uniuscuiusque cistae communi applicentur.

CAP. 27
De Tutorum officio, diligentia, et stipendio

Quoniam ad bene instituendam iuventutem plurimum praesidii in tutorum cura et diligentia constat esse positum: quapropter unumquemque scholarium et pensionariorum collegii praedicti tutorem habere volumus, qui de cuiusque eorum moribus et diligentia rationem sit redditurus, et eos, cum opus erit, diligenter erudiat, praecipue vero religione sincera et vera Dei cognitione imbuat. Tutores autem, qui hanc curam suscipient, neminem nisi Magistrum et socios esse permittimus: ne vero id munus scholares aut pensionarios aut etiam sisatores nimium oneret, volumus ut scholares seu sisatores praedicti nihil omnino pensitent tutoribus suis annui salarii vel mercedis nomine. Pensionarii vero ad mensam et convictum sociorum admissi non ultra quadraginta solidos annuos: caeteri vero pensionarii non ultra viginti sex solidos et octo denarios annuae mercedis et salarii nomine solvere cogentur. Si quis tutorum aliquid nomine praedicto ultra quam est praescriptum acceperit vel exegerit, is, nisi a Magistro admonitus ab huiusmodi exactionibus abstinuerit, ad munus tutoris capessendum nullo modo admittatur: et quos habet suae tutelae commissos, eos Magister aliis tutoribus vel alteri tutori erudiendos committat. Ac ne quis plures quam expediat in suam tutelam accipiat, numeri moderationem Magistro committimus. Itaque nec sociorum quisquam quempiam in suam tutelam accipiet, nisi Magistri consensu: nec numerum maiorem retinebit quam ipsi videbitur expedire. Tutorum praedictorum unumquemque, si duos pluresve pupillos habuerit suae tutelae creditos, duos eorum ad minimum in suo cubiculo cubantes volumus, nisi iustam rationem viderit Magister, cur hunc numerum minuat: qui vero sub cura erunt tutorum, nunquam in oppidum egredientur sine suorum tutorum consensu, nisi cum erunt audiendae lectiones in scholis publicis, aut cum alia exercitia literarum vel conciones publicae habebuntur, aut cum conventus publici in Academia indicentur.

CAP. 28
De lustrandis scholasticorum cubiculis, ne inutiles conventus in eisdem celebrentur

Inter multa incommoda, quae studiosorum in bonis literis progressionem impediunt, non parum nocent adolescentium inter se frequentes de rebus inanibus collocutiones: nam praeter temporis iacturam (quod non in minimis damnis ponendum est) prava innascitur iuvenilibus animis consuetudo, qua a rebus seriis ad nugas et ineptias facillime solent avocari. Statuimus igitur et ordinamus, ut nec pensionarii, nec scholares, nec sisatores, nec subsisatores (nisi qui Magistri artium fuerint) ullos conventus in cubiculis suis aut ludendi, aut epulandi, aut confabulandi gratia, aut quocunque alio nomine celebrare praesumant. Quisquis autem contra fecerit, si adultus fuerit, per Magistrum aut eius absentis vicarium pro singulis vicibus duodecim denarios mulctetur: sin puerilem aetatem non excesserit, verberibus per Decanum castigetur: et quo diligentius ista observentur, statuimus et ordinamus, ut socii, aut singuli aut bini, pro Magistri arbitrio, suo quisque ordine huiusmodi pensionariorum, scholarium, sisatorum, subsisatorum cubicula noctu bis ad minimum singulis septimanis lustrent et invisant; et quid in quoque agatur diligenter explorent, sedulos laudent, negligentes increpent, et quoscunque hoc statutum violare deprehenderint, eorum nomina postridie deferant, quo perinde mulctentur, ut superius est ordinatum: huiusmodi vero delinquentium pecuniariae mulctae sociorum cedant commeatui.

CAP. 29
De Lectore et sublectoribus

Adhuc deesse huic corpori membrum pernecessarium advertimus, quo nova soboles procreari possit; volumus igitur et statuimus, quod per Magistrum et maiorem partem sociorum quispiam ex iis in lectorem domesticum eligatur. Quod officium electus nemo recusabit sub poena amissionis societatis suae, sed diligenter exequi tenebitur, quamdiu Magister et maior pars sociorum illud in commodum collegii cedere iudicarint. Lector autem ipse diebus profestis, iuxta morem Academiae in aliis collegiis observatum (pulsata prius campanula immediate post preces matutinas) lectores palam in aula collegii unius horae spatio praelegentes audiet, auditores, quoties opus fuerit, examinabit, et per sublectores suos examinari diligenter curabit. Quis vero liber in quaque classe, quaque methodo explicandus sit, Magistri et Decani arbitrio relinquimus. At si lector ipse librum aliquem per se exponere velit (quod ipsum aliquando facere praecipimus) quem velit librum eligat, ex Platonis, Aristotelis, aut Ciceronis operibus qua hora, et quamdiu, quibusque anni temporibus praelecturus sit, Magister et maior pars sociorum pro arbitrio suo constituent. Aderit praeterea et moderabitur scholasticis disputationibus et omnibus exercitationibus ab initio usque ad finem, prout ab ipso Magistro et maiori parte sociorum praescriptum fuerit. Atque ne lector nimio onere prematur, sublectores quosdam ex sociis (se fieri possit) aut ex Magistris et Baccalaureis non sociis eligi volumus per Magistrum et maiorem partem sociorum. Quorum quisque officium suum exequatur in persona sua, nisi forte legitima causa impeditus fuerit per Magistrum approbanda: sed et tunc eum substituere suis impensis quendam alium virum idoneum volumus, qui illius vices iudicio Magistri diligenter implebit.

CAP. 30
De Lectorum stipendio

Sed quia iustum est laborem omnem praemia compensari: volumus et statuimus quod lectori singulis anni quartis nomine stipendii tresdecem solidi et quatuor denarii solvantur per Magistrum seu eius locum tenentem praeter alia emolumenta ei per Magistrum et maiorem partem sociorum assignanda. Et propterea volumus et statuimus ut officium suum quisque in singulis antedictis exequatur in persona sua, nisi forte legitima causa impeditus fuerit per Magistrum approbata: tunc autem substituere suis impensis quendam alium ex sociis ad hoc officium praestandum idoneum, qui illius vices iudicio Magistri diligenter implebit. Quod si negotiis ullis implicetur, quae diuturnam absentiam postulant, sive gravi et prolixa aegrotatione afficiatur, aut denique promotionem aliquam sit assequutus, ob quam necesse fuerit ei ius societatis suae amittere, tunc alteri cuidam ex sociis officium ipsum commendari volumus per Magistrum et maiorem partem eorundem. Sublectorum vero stipendia ex ipsius lectoris stipendio iudicio Magistri

et maioris partis sociorum desumentur, et singulis eorum per Magistrum aut eius locum tenentem persolventur.

CAP. 31
De Lectoris authoritate in discipulos

At supervacaneum erit hoc membrum, nisi semen adfuerit unde prodire
nova soboles possit et nasci: volumus igitur et statuimus, ut omnes
huius collegii scholares, necnon pensionarii, in eodem degentes, aliique
quot Magistro et maiori parti sociorum videbuntur necessarii, lecturis
et caeteris exercitationibus scholasticis antedictis diligentem operam
dabunt. Quos lector ipse iuxta prudentiam suam corripiat et mulctet, si
vel tardius quam debent accesserint ad lecturas, aut ad alia scholastica
exercitamenta: sive absentes fuerint ab eisdem, aut praesentes non
diligenter attenderint, pro tarditate quaque, id est, si principio cuiusvis
lecturae suae, sive sophismatis, problematis, oppositionum, examina-
tionum, aut disputationum non adfuerint, quadrante; si ultra medietatem
alicuius eorum abfuerint, obolo; si per universum, denario singulos
discipulos mulctari volumus; et toties quoties in aliquo praedictorum
eos ita delinquere contingerit, si adulti fuerint; alioqui virga corri-
gantur. Quarum mulctarum emolumenta sociorum convictui assignamus. Veruntamen, si lector nimis asperum et durum se praestiterit
cuiquam, iudicio Magistri et senioris socii reformetur. Quod si discipulus quispiam crebro punitus se noluerit emendare, sed magis et
magis deliquerit ac notabiliter, tum lector ipse rem referet Magistro et
maiori parti sociorum, a quibus tertio admonitus, si perrexerit indies in
notabili negligentia sua, illum omni commoditate sua privari volumus
intra collegium praedictum, et in perpetuum excludi.

CAP. 32
De scholarium discipulorum qualitate et electione

Ne sit ergo seminarium ineptum et manui inobediens, nec quod molliter
et generose tractari possit, volumus et statuimus ut discipulorum electio
fiat ex illis iuvenibus qui pauperiores, probiores, aptiores atque egregii
magis fuerint, quique sint probitate, indole ac bona spe, nec Baccalaurei
in artibus, nec ad sacrum ministerium admissi, quique sacram Theo-
logiam ac ministerium sanctum proposuerunt sibi, sintque (saltem

mediocriter) instructi et periti in Graecis, Rhetorica, et Logica: in-
digentes tamen inprimis, modo caeteris conditionibus fuerint pares. Ob
quod et illos praecipue, qui de comitatu Essexiae et Northamptoniae
oriundi sunt, praeponi volumus; de quibus duos scholares semper esse
volumus in ipso collegio; ita tamen ut non plures tribus ex aliquo
praedictorum sive ex alio ullo comitatu totius Angliae pro discipulis
uno tempore habeantur. Modum vero in discipulis eligendis et examin-
andis eundem observari volumus, quem in statutis de sociorum electione et illam antecedentibus descripsimus.

CAP. 33
De iureiurando scholarium discipulorum

Et quoniam universis sanctum iuramentum violare maxime verendum
est, idcirco volumus et statuimus, quod scholarium discipulorum
unusquisque mox post electionem suam, et antequam alicuius emolu-
menti intra dictum collegium particeps admittatur, iuret, tactis sacrosanctis Dei Evangeliis, in praesentia Magistri et maioris partis sociorum,
in hac forma:

Ego N.N. Deum testor, quod Statuta omnia et singula quae Gualtherus Mildmaius, fundator huius collegii, pro eodem administrando
per se edidit, veraciter et integre observabo, quoad in me fuerit, et
quatenus meam personam concernunt, et ab aliis itidem fieri enitar.
Magistro sive eius locum tenenti in cunctis parebo, quaecunque legitime
praeceperit. Consilia collegii (si quae audivero non efferenda) secreta
tenebo. Sociis omnibus et singulis reverentiam iustam et honorem
exhibebo; nihil denique quod aut in dedecus aut incommodum Magistro
sive sociorum alicui aut collegio ipsi verti posse credidero, conabor, sed
neque conantibus ipse ullo modo consentiam, quoad vixero. Haec
omnia in me recipio, quatenus statutis regni editis aut edendis non
repugnent, et hoc iureiurando polliceor, quatenus me Deus adiuvet per
Jesum Christum.

CAP. 34
De cultu Dei, scholasticis exercitationibus, et moribus discipulorum

Nihil iuveni fugiendum magis inerti otio; et propterea volumus et
statuimus ut discipulus quisque aut in cultu Dei, aut bonarum artium
studiis, aut moribus egregiis producendis, semper, quoad fieri possit,
sit occupatus: diebus omnibus Dominicis et caeteris diebus publicarum

precum absque ulla exceptione divinorum officiorum cuique integre adesse volumus in sacello eiusdem collegii. Lecturis etiam omnibus et caeteris exercitamentis scholasticis universis, tam quae domi fuerint, quam foris in scholis publicis, intererit quisque iuxta captum et annos suos ac morem ipsius universitatis; quo possit merito et digne suo tempore, etiam quamprimum ipsius universitatis statuta sinunt, gradus suscipere. Socios etiam et scholares praedictos tam domi quam foris modeste et honeste se gerere volumus; contentionibus et rixis abstinere; in concionibus publicis audiendis frequentes esse; modestiam omnem vultu, gestu corporis et vestitus genere et forma praeferre; literis sic diligenter incumbere, ut fructu ipso diligentiam suam contestentur: quod si qui in praemissis Magistri iudicio minime probabitur, tunc a Magistro cum assistentia Decani admonitum, ut mores, vestitus genus et formam vel negligentiam emendet, nisi sic correxerit se, ut eiusdem Magistri iudicio videatur emendatus, communias illi subtrahi tamdiu volumus quoad se correxerit; quod si secundo et tertio admonitus secundum formam praedictam non paruerit, vel in emendatione vitiorum et negligentiarum Magistri iudicio non satisfecerit, tum ad causam dicendam coram Magistro et sociis in collegio praesentetur, et si ita videbitur Magistro et maiori parti sociorum, iure societatis vel scholariatus vel pensionariatus sine ulla ulteriore appellatione vel querela in perpetuum privari volumus.

CAP. 35
De obsequiis intra Collegium exhibendis

Et ne nimiis forte in Magistrum et socios obsequiis scholares ab eruditione impediantur, volumus et statuimus, quod nec Magister nec sociorum aliquis quenquam scholarium ad ulla obsequia sibi praestanda urgeat, aut ad negotia aliqua pro collegio obeunda, praeterquam in prandiis, coenis et biberiis, intra aulam ipsium collegii, aut divinorum officiorum tempore intra sacellum eiusdem, in quibus sex aut plures aut pauciores (pro Magistri arbitrio) eorum singulis hebdomadis iuxta cursus et ordines suos obsequi volumus, et ministrare pro mensa sociorum in his rebus quae ad illam pertinent introferendis aut efferendis diligenter, et pro legendis Bibliis ante et post prandium et coenam. Caeteris vero temporibus eruditioni suae et bonis artibus intendant, quo iure possint gradus scholasticos, quamprimum tempus legitimum advenerit, assequi. Nam neminem diutius intra collegium dictum pro scholari discipulo haberi volumus, postquam illi semel per suos annos gradum Magisterii in artibus suscipere licuerit. Quod si Magistro et maiori parti sociorum obsequia praedicta vel eorum aliquod per alios quam scholares dicti collegii obeunda esse videbuntur, statuimus ut aliis pro temporum et personarum ratione liceat eis eadem obsequia permittere et imponere.

CAP. 36

Quantum a Collegio, quantumve ab aliis scholares
discipuli recipient, et de eorum absentia

Et quo discipuli isti acrius incitentur ad studia, volumus et statuimus quod singulis hebdomadis pro uniuscuiusque eorum communiis duodecim denarii Senescallo tribuantur, quam summam ab ipso collegio acceperint ad duo anni tempora consuetudinaria: illam vero (quoad eius fieri potest) nolumus communias eorum supergredi: si tamen supergressae fuerint summam illam, quicquid deerit, singuli discipulorum ex suo ipsius argento senescallo persolvere teneantur, vicissim recepturi, cum communiae minores fuerint, quicquid erit residui; ac pro vestitura annua quatuordecim solidos et octo denarios; cuius vestiturae certum quendam colorem a Magistro assignari volumus. Considere etiam una omnes volumus in prandiis et coenis intra aulam ipsius collegii ad mensas pro eis deputatas; quaternos in singulis cameris cubare, et non plures, et si quispiam eorum donatus fuerit re aliqua, unde redditus annuus illi tribuatur ultra valorem octo marcarum, aut beneficio quocunque quod animarum curam sibi annexam habeat, singulis emolumentis post pacificam ipsius possessionem immediate vacare volumus: et demum nemini ex illis licere per noctem aut diem integrum a collegio ipso abesse absque Magistri aut locum eius tenentis concessione: neque ultra viginti dies unius anni, nisi iustam et necessariam causam illi esse Magister aut eius locum tenens et maior pars sociorum approbaverit: pro tempore etiam absentiae nihil cuivis allocari debere, ut de sociis ante statuimus.

CAP. 37

De Mancipe, Cocis, lotore, et quodam Magistri famulo

Postremo quosdam intra collegium dictum advertimus discipulis ipsis inferiores, famulos videlicet et mercenarios, quos universo corpori pedum loco habendos esse iudicamus; de quibus aliquid statuere non erit supervacaneum.

Principio Mancipem quendam esse volumus, qui ex consilio Senescalli panem, potum et esculenta providebit praedicto corpori necessaria, quique claves panarii et promptuarii gestabit, cuique, cum opus erit, ministraturus. Cum pistoribus et pandoxatoribus, hebdomadis singulis, computabit; librum quoque consulto Senescallo in exitu cuiusque hebdomadae conficiet pro communiarum computo: et claves denique portarum omnium collegii tam anteriorum quam posteriorum (ipsis ad horam noctis debitam obseratis) Magistro deferet sive eius locum tenenti. Caeterum quo diligentius agat haec omnia, pro stipendio suscipere eum volumus singulis anni quartis sex solidos, denarios octo, praeter communias scholares et emolumenta moderata, quae non pauca exsurgent, e computo pistoris, pandoxatorum, atque carnificum, nisi Magister aliquid ex praedictis emolumentis iustis de causis detrahendum iudicaverit in usus collegii conferendum. Erit et coquus unus primarius pro parandis eduliis, qui praeter negotia coquina mancipem iuvabit in esculentorum emptione, suscipietque in stipendium singulis anni quartis solidos sex et denarios octo praeter communias scholares et emolumenta coquina ad eum pertinentia. Alius ei substituetur subcoquus, qui subministrabit, et vasa coquinaria singula expurgabit; cuius stipendium erit pro communiis duodecim denarii singulis hebdomadis, et alia emolumenta culinaria, quae subcoquo in collegio Christi conceduntur. Neque minus necessarium ut collegii vestes omnes lineae, quibus in mensis uti necesse est, singula quaque hebdomada laventur: idcirco volumus, ut vir quispiam ad hoc officium idoneus provideatur honestae et bonae conversationis; qui pro stipendiis, singulis anni quartis, recipiet sex solidos et octo denarios; neminemque supradictorum stipendiariorum conduci volumus sine consensu Magistri et maioris partis sociorum: et quendam, praeter hos, famulum Magistro permittimus ad sua negotia peculiaria, cuius stipendium antea assignavimus.

CAP. 38
Da praesentationibus ad ecclesias vacantes faciendis

Magnum solicitudinis onus imponunt ii, qui, quarum essent ipsi ecclesiarum patroni, eas, ut quam optimis pastoribus traderentur, freti Magistri sociorumque fide atque iudicio, huic nostro collegio commendarunt vel commendaturi sunt. Quamobrem ut et illorum piis

voluntatibus opinionique satisfiat, et iis etiam consulatur, quorum
certum est animarum salutem ab illarum ecclesiarum religiosa insti-
tutione non minima ex parte pendere, Magistrum et socios in Domino
hortamur, ut in pastoribus harum ecclesiarum designandis, et quarum
etiam posthac erit eodem exemplo solicitudo in ipsos ab earum patronis
reiecta, sincere versentur, et neque gratiam in ea re cuiusquam respiciant
neque muneribus moveantur; sed quem teste conscientia sua existima-
bunt iis maxime ornatum dotibus, quas Spiritus Sanctus vero pastori
ascribit, in eum suffragia sua conferant, statuantque, quicquid hic a
scientibus peccatum erit, eius errati apud summum Judicem, ut de
prodito fratrum sanguine, rationem sibi esse aliquando reddendam. Et
quo totum hoc eligendorum pastorum negotium accuratius adminis-
tretur, volumus et statuimus, ut infra trium mensium spatium ab eo
tempore, quo scient alicui ex ecclesiis praedictis pastorem deesse (sive
id morte eius, qui ultimus in eo munere fuit, sive deprivatione, sive
resignatione, vel quovis alio modo acciderit) aliquem ex suo numero
eligant, quem maxime statuent esse idoneum, quique nullum habeat
aliud beneficium ecclesiasticum, cui animarum curam aut residendi
necessitatem assiduitatemve leges, statuta, aut consuetudines huius
regni, vel beneficii ipsius fundatio, vel locale statutum, aut consuetudo
annexuerunt, eumque Dioceseos illius Episcopo, in qua erit vacans
ecclesia, vel alteri cuicunque instituendi pastoris sive rectoris potestatem habenti, cum effectu praesentent, ab ipso in pastorem sive
rectorem ecclesiae praedictae admittendum et instituendum. Aliunde
vero sumi, quos in pastores seu rectores ecclesiarum praesentabunt,
quam ex ipso collegio (cum suffecturum illud ad viros ad hoc munus
idoneos suppeditandum non dubitemus) omnino prohibemus.

Volumus etiam et statuimus, ut nemo ad curam vacantis ecclesiae
obeundam praesentetur, nisi qui prius cautionem idoneam Magistro et
sociis collegii praedicti praestiterit, se quoad pastoris vel rectoris in ea
ecclesia, ad quam praesentabitur, locum obtinebit, residentiam assiduam
ex iuris publici praescripto in praedicta ecclesia facturum; nec dispensationem aliquam, quae eum a residendi necessitate liberet, obten-
turum vel etiam admissurum; beneficium quoque nullum ecclesiasticum,
dignitatem vel officium, quae annexam habebunt curam animarum, vel
quae eum ad residentiam vel assiduitatem extra ecclesiam praedictam
astringent (statutis aut consuetudinibus huius regni, fundatione,
statuto, vel consuetudine locali ita fortasse exigentibus) quoad erit
illius ecclesiae pastor aut rector, accepturum vel retenturum. Denique,

ut sordes omnes ab hoc negotio amoveantur, omniaque pie religioseque pro causae ipsius gravitate tractentur, volumus et statuimus ut, si Magister, aut sociorum collegii praedicto quispiam pro suffragio suo in praesentatione pastoris ad aliquam ecclesiarum praedictarum ferendo, vel etiam pro suffragio in aliquem collato pecuniam vel munus aliud quodcunque accepisse convincetur, locum, quem in collegio praedicto obtinet, perpetuo amittat. Advocationes cuiquam concedendi Magistro et sociis omnem facultatem penitus praescindimus, ut et impropriationibus assentiendi potestatem.

CAP. 39

De Stipendiis, aliisque allocationibus, Magistro, sociis, et scholaribus, necnon caeteris Collegii ministris, pro incremento reddituum augendis

Quanquam stipendia Magistri, Sociorum, Scholarium, caeterorumque ministrorum, et quid cuique quotidiani victus allocandum est, antea praescripserimus; quia tamen ea pro praesenti ratione reddituum collegii praedicti moderari coacti sumus (uberiora libenter facturi, si praedicti redditus suppeterent) speramus fore, ut bonorum virorum liberalitate in posterum sic augeantur, ut sit unde ad liberaliorem allocationem dictis Magistro, sociis, et scholaribus, et caeteris ministris faciendam suppetat. Volumus igitur et statuimus, ut, si redditus annuus dicti collegii quoquomodo in posterum auctiores reddi contigerit, stipendia allocationesque caeterae, quae Magistro, sociis, et scholaribus, et caeteris ministris fiant virtute ordinationum nostrarum praedictarum, pro portione incrementi reddituum praedictorum, habitaque ratione conditionis cuiusque eorum augeantur: ita tamen ut quod Magistro concedetur, non excedat annuam summam quadraginta librarum, nec quod assignabitur cuiquam ex sociis praedictis, excedat summam annuam decem librarum, nec scholarium cuiquam amplius tribuatur, quam summa annua quatuor librarum, nec stipendia ministrorum praedictorum cuiusquam excedat summam quadraginta solidorum, nisi aliter visum fuerit Fundatori praedicto, quoad in hac vita fuerit. Nolumus tamen, ut stipendia vel allocationes praedictae prius augeantur, quam ad eum modum auctae sint collegii facultates, ut ad Magistrum duodecim socios, triginta scholares, quibus aequa caeteris stipendia et allocationes fiant, quo modo antea est praescriptum, sufficere possunt una cum decem pauperibus ad mensam sociorum ministraturis, et ex

reliquiis eiusdem mensae victuris, quibus singulis dabuntur praeterea
de redditibus collegii nostri singulae drachmae hebdomadatim. Cum
numerus scholarium ad quadraginta excreverit, tum Magister pro
stipendio et allocationibus suis accipiet quinquaginta libras: si vero
praedictus scholarium numerus ad quinquaginta excreverit, tum accipiet
sexaginta libras.

CAP. 40

De Pensionariis intra Collegium admittendis

Circumspicientes adhuc unde perniciem aut malum aliquod huic
corpori oriri queat, non videmus id facile fieri posse ex membris ipsis,
cum tam exacta cuiusque personae, priusquam in illum numerum
recipiatur, probatio habenda est. Maximum ergo quod veremur, est, si
quosdam praeter hunc numerum convivas et pensionarios admittant,
quorum non integra conversatio alios forte corrumpet; atque ita
sensim universi reliqui corporis labes sequatur.

Volumus igitur et statuimus, quod nemo alius ut pensionarius
admittatur ad convictum et conversandum in dicto collegio, nisi qui
testimonio Magistri et maioris partis sociorum probatae vitae ac famae
inviolatae fuerit: quique aut scholaribus, sociis, aut discipulis in moribus
probis excolendis, actibus scholasticis exercendis, et divinis officiis
celebrandis se conformaturum fideliter promiserit coram Magistro et
maiore parte sociorum, et hisce nostris statutis et legibus obtempera-
turum, priusquam intra dictum collegium admittantur. Neque quenquam pensionariorum praedictorum diutius in collegio morari
permittimus, quam ut scholastica exercitia, quae caeteris suae conditionis imponantur, diligenter obeat, et moribus talis esse perseveret,
ut Magistri iudicio probetur. Nullum etiam pro pensionario ad convictum scholarium aut sociorum admitti vel in collegio morari volumus,
qui beneficium aliquod nactus est, curam animarum habens annexam:
quique non cameram habet, uti in dicto collegio cubet. Ad mensam
vero et convictum sociorum neminem admitti volumus, nisi in artibus
Magistrum vel Baccalaureum in sacra Theologia, aut Professorem, vel
qui non sit filius Militis, seu Equitis aurati, aut alterius viri, maioris
nobilitatis gradu insignis, nisi ex iusta et idonea Magistro collegii et
maiori parti sociorum probanda causa. Famulum praeterea nulli ex
sociis dicti collegii vel ex pensionariis ad mensam et sociorum convictum admissis habere licere permittimus, nisi famulus cameram habeat
in collegio, et literis operam det, obeatque omnia exercitia, quae

scholaribus et pensionariis praescribentur pro cuiusque in literis progressu et facultate. Pensionarios etiam quaternos in uno cubiculo cubare volumus, nisi aliter Magistro visum fuerit iustis de causis duobus ad minimum cubiculum unum assignare. Pensionarii, ad sociorum convictum admissi, singulis anni quartis solvent duos solidos in usus necessarios insumendos pro Magistri et maioris partis sociorum arbitrio; qui autem ad scholarium convictum admittuntur, duodecim denarios singulis anni quartis.

CAP. 41

De ambiguis et obscuris interpretandis

Quod si quid obscuri in his nostris statutis emerserit, quod interpretationem necessariam desideret, interpretationem eius nobis ipsis (quoad in hac vita fuerimus) reservamus, eaque contentos esse Magistrum, socios et scholares praedictos, et pro statuto illius collegii perpetuo habere et observare volumus; postquam autem nos Deus pro sua misericordia ex hac vita evocaverit, tum si quid postea emerserit ambigui et obscuri, de eo Magistrum et socios in collegio praesentes tractare volumus, et interpretationem, quam ipsorum pars maior fecerit, pro vera et legitima haberi et teneri. Quod si inter ipsos modo praedictos non convenerit, vel si quispiam ex sociis vel scholaribus interpretationem illam iniquam esse queretur, tunc intra decem dies a tempore tractatus praedicti Magistrum collegii Christi et duos seniores in sacra Theologia Doctores universitatis praedictae adiri volumus, et quam sententiam statuti controversi duo ipsorum esse decreverint, ex ea volumus controversiam praedictam terminari, omnesque in eadem acquiescere.

CAP. 42

De communi omnium conditione qui erunt in collegio

Quanquam eum honorem coniugio libenter deferimus, quem ei spiritus sanctus in sacris literis tribuit, eorumque reprobamus sententias, qui certo hominum ordini matrimonium censuerunt interdicendum: multae tamen sunt et graves causae, cur neminem eorum, qui in membris collegii nostri censebuntur, maritos esse patiamur. Volumus igitur et statuimus, ut sive quis posthac in collegium cooptabitur, qui uxorem habeat, eius electio, tanquam omnis iuris in collegio praedicto incapacis, irrita habeatur: sive post admissionem suam uxorem duxerit, ius omne quod per electionem huiusmodi consequutus sit, in perpetuum amittat.

Atque haec Statuta pro administrando collegio nostro edidimus, et ab omnibus eius membris diligenter et inviolate observari praecipimus: ita tamen, ut nobis reservemus authoritatem, quamdiu in hac vita manserimus, addendi, detrahendi, mutandi, et interpretandi, quotiescunque iustas causas oblatas viderimus. In quorum omnium fidem et testimonium Ego, supranominatus Gualtherus Mildmaius, praesentibus sigillum meum apposui.

Datum primo die Octobris, anno Domini millesimo quingentesimo octuagesimo quinto, et anno Illustrissimae Dominae Elizabethae, Angliae, Franciae et Hiberniae Reginae etc. vicesimo septimo.

WA: MILDMAY.

Statuta, superius in hoc libro contenta, confirmata fuerunt per honorandum virum Dominum Walterum Mildmaium, et ab eodem subscripta, sigilloque suo consignata: ac deinde Laurentio Chaddertono, magistro Collegii Emanuelis in Academia Cantabrigiensi, pro Statutis dicti collegii tradita Nobis praesentibus.

ANT. MILDMAY.   HUM. MILDMAY.
JO. HAMMOND.   THO. BYNG.
W. LEWYN.   TIMOTHE BRIGHT.
                EDMUND DOWNYNGE.

Statutum De Camera Consanguineis fundatoris reservanda

Cum natura omnibus praecipuum quendam amorem ingeneraverit in eos, quos aut ipsi propagarunt, aut sibi habent sanguinis necessitudine coniunctos, curandum putavimus, ut quod sine literarum detrimento fieri potuit, etiam in hoc collegio stirpis et familiae nostrae aliquam videremus habuisse rationem. Quamobrem unicam cameram ex earum numero, quae recens extructae sunt, quaeque in eo ordine extrema Orientem respicit, et inter imam cameram et supremam tecto proximam interiacet, posteris et Consanguineis nostris, qui studii causa in collegium praedictum asciscentur, dicandam esse censuimus. Volumus itaque et statuimus, ut si quis unus vel plures ex iis qui de nostro erunt cognomine, et simul nostra vel Agnatorum nostrorum stirpe propagabuntur, in collegio praedicto quandocunque in posterum studii causa degent, iis camera praedicta deferatur, eaque solus vel soli gratis et libere fruantur, quoad in eo collegio manebunt, nulla repensione vel mercede pro eadem dependenda. Quod si nulli erunt in collegio praedicto nobis agnati, et eodem nobiscum cognomine, tunc si quis erit ex filiarum nostrarum stirpe, aut per eas nobis sanguine coniunctus, vel si ea qualitate plures erunt, tunc cameram praedictam ab illo vel illis, quoad in dicto collegio literarum causa morabuntur, sine ulla solutione pensionis vel mercedis similiter volumus obtineri et occupari. Quibus vero temporibus nullum ita, ut praediximus, nobis coniunctum in collegio praedicto esse contigerit, liberam facimus Magistro collegii praedicti potestatem eandem cameram alii cuicunque in eodem collegio studii causa versanti, dum dignitatis meritorumque personae ac aequitatis habeat rationem, suo arbitrio assignandi. Volumus tamen, ut a nostro sanguine alienus sub hac conditione ad cameram praedictam et non aliter admittatur, ut de eadem discedat, cum primum aliquis ex eorum numero, quos praeferendos esse ostendimus, in collegium praedictum studii causa admittetur et recipietur, eandemque statim ei cedat, per eum, quoad in eo collegio fuerit, gratis obtinendam, quam etiam eidem in eo casu assignari et concedi, nonobstante concessione eiusdem alteri prius facta, vigore praesentis Statuti, volumus et mandamus. December, 1587.

WA: MILDMAY.

De mora sociorum in Collegio, et de gradu Doctoratus in
sacra Theologia Suscipiendo

Cum eo consilio collegium nostrum fundaverimus, ut esset per Dei gratiam doctorum virorum seminarium, unde suppetat Ecclesiae, quanta inde maxima exhiberi possit copia, ad populum Christiana religione imbuendum, nolumus sociorum quenquam existimare sibi in isto collegio perpetuum habitandi domicilium a nobis esse datum; idque eo magis cavendum arbitramur, quod multorum prudentium et gravium virorum querelis interfuerimus, qui multis suae memoriae praesentibusque confirmarint exemplis, nimium diuturnam sociorum in aliis collegiis moram communes reipublicae et ecclesiae utilitates non mediocriter afflixisse. Nam cum ipsi interea pene inutiles sint, tum fructum eum, qui ab aliorum laudabili industria copiosior expectari poterit, reipublicae eripiunt. Ut ergo in isto proventu literatorum hominum, quem cupimus esse amplissimum, ubertatis rationem habuisse videamur, unaque etiam dignitati et existimationi collegii nostri consulamus, volumus et statuimus, ut tam Magister collegii praedicti, quam socii omnes praesentes et futuri ad gradum Doctoratus in sacra Theologia, quamprimum per publica Academiae statuta possint licebitve, se curent promoveri. Si quis vero ipsorum, sive Magister, sive sociorum quisquam, eo temporis spatio quod ad illum gradum statutis est praefixum, Doctoratus in sacra Theologia gradum non obtinuerit, tunc a die Comitiorum, quo proximo Doctoratus insignia accipere alioqui potuisset, locum quem habet habebitque in collegio, perpetuo amittat. Suscepto autem semel gradu praedicto, Magistrum quidem ipsum perpetuum esse volumus. Sociorum vero nullum a die Comitiorum, quo erit Doctor solenni ritu creatus, vel speciali gratia doctoratum actualem susceperit, ultra annum socii locum volumus retinere. In isto tamen anno tempus totum illud, quo ipsorum quenquam aut Procancellariatus munus obire, aut Regii in sacra Theologia, eiusve quem illustrissima domina Margareta Comitissa Richemundiae et Darbeiae instituit, lectoris munere fungi contigerit (modo id suo iure et nomine faciant) nolumus omnino numerari. Cum primum autem magistratu abierint, vel lectorum illorum quos descripsimus locum tenere desierint, tunc decursis diebus, qui, subducto magistratus sui vel legendi tempore, anno explendo superfuerunt, socii in perpetuum esse desinant. Ne tamen, qui ista ratione a collegio nostro recedant, arbitrentur se a nobis prorsus abdicatos, volumus et statuimus, ut quandocunque beneficium aliquod ad ius Patronatus nostri collegii spectans post cuiusquam eorum discessum vacare contigerit, liceat Magistro et sociis dicti collegii eundem ad dictum beneficium perinde (si ita iis videbitur) praesentare, ac si ius socii adhuc retinuisset: dum tamen eo tempore aliud beneficium ecclesiasticum, quod curam animarum habeat annexam, non obtineat, aut quod habeat cum effectu dimittat, et nullum antea beneficium ex praesentatione collegii acceperit. Et ne tum quidem volumus eius rationem haberi, nisi eodem prorsus modo, quo de sociis ad beneficia praesentandis antea est a nobis statutum, caveat se aliud beneficium curatum, quodve residentiam personalem exigat, nisi eo, quod praesentante collegio obtinebit, penitus dimisso, non accepturum, et residentiam ex iuris publici praescripto in eo, quoad id obtinebit, esse facturum. Ne autem de Doctoratu in sacra Theologia solum solliciti fuisse, caeteros vero gradus Scholasticos neglexisse existimemur, volumus et statuimus, ut si quis sociorum collegii nostri praedicti eo temporis spatio, quod est ad eam rem statutis Academiae praefinitum, Magister in artibus, aut in sacra Theologia Baccalaureus non fuerit, tunc proximis Comitiis, quibus ex more ii gradus candidatis deferuntur, elapsis, a collegio penitus amoveatur, spe omni societatis nova electione iterum in dicto collegio assequendae in perpetuum illi praecisa. Eandemque volumus esse conditionem magistri sociorumque omnium, quos quacunque ex causa loco suo amovendos esse aliis nostris statutis continetur.

Datum ultimo die Februarii, Anno Domini millesimo quingentesimo octuagesimo septimo, et Anno illustrissimae Dominae Elizabethae, Angliae, Franciae et Hiberniae Reginae, etc. tricesimo.

WA: MILDMAY.

Index

rents, *see*: room-rents
residence
  of Fellows, 62, 66f.
  of incumbents of College livings, 82f.
  of Scholars, 79
  see also: *De mora sociorum* statute
Richardson, John, 99, 100
Ridley, Nicholas, 9, 13
ritual
  at Christ's College, 8
  movement against, 13, 14
Rolfe, Richard, 99, 100
room-rents, 32, 49

St John's College, foundation of, 6f.
sanitation, 104
Scholars
  duties of in Hall and Chapel, 78
  election of, 74
  to be intending ordinands, 74
  selected by the Founder, 18
  and Tutors, 68
sermons, *see*: preaching
Sidney Sussex College, 97
sizars, 68, 69, 78
social origins of students, 6, 7, 12
sophismata, 50
sports, field, 62
statutes of the realm, 75
Statutes, University, 14, 76
Steward, 51, 79

stipends
  Fellows' 63, 64, 84
  Master's, 37, 84
  Scholars', 79, 84
  Tutors', 68, 84
study
  choice of books for, 70, 101, 102
  subjects of, 5, 9, 52, 60, 74
  times of, 28, 104f.
sub-sizars, 68, 69, 78
surplices, 76f.
suspension (from Fellowship), 40

tablecloths, 80, 81
treasury, 33, 35
Trinity College, 10, 11
Tutors, 7, 68

uniformity, religious, 12, 14, 109–12

visitation of students' rooms, 69, 100, 101
visitor, office not prescribed for
      Emmanuel, 17, 88
  see also: appeals

Walsingham, Sir Francis, 29
Westmorland Building, 94
Westmorland, Earls of, descended from
      Sir Walter Mildmay, 23
women, exclusion from College, 62, 89

Zwingli, 111